History *of* Buddhist
HUMANISM

Published by

World Tribune Press
606 Wilshire Blvd.
Santa Monica, CA 90401

Front cover photo © iStockphoto
Cover and interior design by Lightbourne, Inc.

This book is printed on Glatfelter Thor PCW paper.
It contains 30% post-consumer waste and is
SFI (Sustainable Forestry Initiative) certified.

Printed in the United States of America.

ISBN: 978-1-935523-15-4

10 9 8 7 6 5 4 3 2

Contents

Editor's Note

The Soka Gakkai recently marked its eightieth year, but it is part of a much longer history, stretching back to the day that Shakyamuni Buddha left his palace and began seeking the truth. The Buddha's vow—for all people to establish absolute happiness and wisdom in their lives—is the core of Buddhist humanism, and the same as the vow for kosen-rufu shared by members of the Soka Gakkai International.

In 2008, Middleway Press reprinted *The Living Buddha: An Interpretive Biography*, SGI President Daisaku Ikeda's 1973 book on the life of Shakyamuni Buddha. President Ikeda's *Buddhism: the First Millennium* and *The Flower of Chinese Buddhism* followed. These three insightful history books inspired the staff of *Living Buddhism* to create a yearlong history series titled "The History of Buddhist Humanism" drawing heavily from those books, as well as from *The Wisdom of the Lotus Sutra* and other sources authored by the SGI president.

Living Buddhism illustrated through this series the ways in which the members of the Buddhist order had at times threatened or subverted— and at other times renewed and revitalized—the fundamental vow of the Buddha. The series begins with the life of Shakyamuni and then focuses on the heritage of ideals and actions of Buddhist reformers such as Nagarjuna, Tiantai Zhiyi, Miole Zhanran and Dengyo—all of whom Nichiren Daishonin considered exemplary Buddhists. The series concludes with a section devoted to showing how the SGI's efforts to realize the Buddha's vow have resulted in the humanistic teachings of Nichiren Buddhism spreading throughout the world.

Due to concerns about the length of each installment, *Living Buddhism* did not give a full account of the life of Nichiren Daishonin or the history of the SGI in its "History of Buddhist Humanism" series. However, to provide a more complete history, this volume includes a two-part article on the life of Nichiren Daishonin and a three-part history of the Soka Gakkai.

SGI President Ikeda welcomes a young friend who has traveled from abroad, Tokyo, May 2008.

Humanism, the Cornerstone of Buddhism

The following are excerpts about Buddhist humanism from SGI President Ikeda's lectures.

Humanism is the cornerstone of Buddhism, the crystallization of the wisdom of the East. Shakyamuni, the founder of Buddhism, describes the age in which he lived as follows: "Seeing people struggling, like fish, writhing in shallow water with enmity against one another, I became afraid" (*Suttanipata*). India, in what would seem to parallel conditions in the world today, was then at a chaotic turning point in its history and had yet to arrive at peace and stability. Spurred by impatience and animosity, people turned in vain to violence. It is said that not even at home could they feel safe without weapons.

Why do people fight? And why must they suffer? With his penetrating eye, Shakyamuni fixed his gaze on the true aspect of the human being, the unchanging reality that is concealed within the transient phenomena of life. He gave himself over to pondering the matter of how the luminance inherent in human life could be brought to shine forth in a radiation of peace, happiness and compassion. In this inquiry lies the starting point of Buddhism. (*My Dear Friends in America*, second edition, pp. 333–34)

· ✳ ·

> *Buddhism is a teaching of unparalleled humanism that stresses the boundless potential within human beings.*

The point where Buddhism radically departs from many other philosophies and religions is that it uncovered within the individual's own life the Law, or limitless inner power, for resolving all suffering on the most essential level. A Buddha is one who, based on this Law, has attained the ultimate wisdom to fundamentally put an end to suffering and construct indestructible happiness.

Buddhism is a teaching of unparalleled humanism that stresses the boundless potential within human beings. That's why it is called the "internal way."

To "perceive the mystic truth that is originally inherent in all living beings" is to "attain unsurpassed enlightenment"; it is the sole means for freeing oneself from "the sufferings of birth and death endured since time without beginning." This is Shakyamuni's starting point, and the entirety of Buddhist thought. The scripture that proclaims this philosophy of the "internal way" is the Lotus Sutra, which teaches that all people can attain enlightenment. The Lotus Sutra could be said to embody the ultimate principle of respect for human dignity. (September–October 2006 *Living Buddhism*, p. 88)

When there is serious confusion regarding the Buddhist teachings in which people place their faith with mistaken beliefs and tenets imperiling the spiritual welfare of society, nothing could be farther from Buddhist compassion than not taking action to rectify the situation. The schools that spread such confusion have forgotten Buddhism's original spirit of working for the people's welfare and helping them gain enlightenment. If their errors were allowed to go unchallenged, it would only plunge people into even greater suffering. Such permissiveness may seem like moderation and tolerance—free of any hint of "a contentious heart"—but remaining passive when faced with error is actually an extremely grave offense. (March–April 2006 *Living Buddhism*, p. 89)

As the scriptures continually remind us, the teachings of the Buddha are intended to bring salvation to all sentient beings. Thus, the early disciples, in compiling the canon, were not simply putting together a record of Shakyamuni's words and actions; they were speaking and acting in his stead. If they themselves had not been able to enter into the same lofty state of mind as the Buddha, they could not have understood Shakyamuni's teachings nor could they have handed them down to later ages. This is why we say that each word and phrase of the sutras represents the golden sayings of the Buddha. And when we, as followers of Buddhism, stand with the scriptures in hand and challenge the society of our time, we too, like the disciples some two thousand years ago, must enter into the same state of mind as the Buddha himself. We must give ourselves wholly to the task of bringing light to the masses of men and women who are lost in suffering and teaching them the true way of life. (*Buddhism: the First Millennium*, pp. 15–16)

No matter how people may insist they have attained enlightenment, if they do not behave compassionately, then they are lying. Wisdom is invisible. A person's conduct, therefore, is the yardstick or barometer for gauging his or her wisdom. The purpose of the Buddha's appearance in the world, after all, is accomplished through his behavior as a human being. (*The Wisdom of the Lotus Sutra*, vol. 2, p. 79)

The Lotus Sutra from beginning to end teaches the oneness, or shared commitment, of mentor and disciple. Looking over the history of Buddhism, the deification of Shakyamuni began when his disciples forgot to strive with the same commitment he had. If Shakyamuni who attained enlightenment in the remote past is turned into a transcendent, superhuman being, then the mentor–disciple relationship cannot function. The point is that when the Buddha's disciples fail to emulate his spirit and conduct, the Buddha merely becomes an object of veneration or worship. The Buddha therefore can no longer serve as a model for others' human revolution.

The Lotus Sutra reveals that a vow lies at the core of Shakyamuni Buddha's character. It further clarifies that the Law is transmitted to disciples who make that vow their own and strive in the same spirit. This paves the way for conveying the life-state of the Buddha to living beings even in the age after his passing. (*The Heritage of the Ultimate Law of Life: SGI President Ikeda's Lecture Series*, p. 93)

Nichiren Buddhism is a religion of kosen-rufu. Without determination and practical efforts to spread the Mystic Law, the Daishonin's teaching becomes nothing but empty words. For a period of seven hundred years, that teaching certainly existed in the form of written words, but it was never spread far and wide. It was our great predecessor Tsunesaburo Makiguchi who revived the Daishonin's teaching in accord with the Daishonin's spirit.

In that sense, the Soka Gakkai's appearance testifies to the validity of Nichiren Buddhism. In the present age, the only place where one can engage in the correct practice of Nichiren Buddhism and encounter the essence of the Daishonin's spirit is in the Soka Gakkai. I wish to declare this as the solemn truth. (July 2002 *Living Buddhism*, p. 18)

· ❀ ·

"After his passing" [See *The Lotus Sutra and Its Opening and Closing Sutras*, p. 203] refers to a time when the Buddha's spirit has been forgotten and there is great turmoil and confusion in areas of religion and philosophy. In such an age, while people might appear to revere the Buddha, they forget the Buddha's essential spirit; and while there are Buddhist schools, the spirit of the Buddha does not abide in them. In such a time, while there may be religions, they exist for the sake of religion and not for human beings. The Lotus Sutra was taught especially for the people of such an age.

The teachers of the Law propagate the Lotus Sutra, which conveys the Buddha's spirit, in an age that has completely forgotten the spirit of the Buddha. Consequently, there is much hatred and jealousy toward them. In an age that has lost sight of humanity, it is no easy undertaking to campaign for a restoration of humanity. (*The Wisdom of the Lotus Sutra,* vol. 2, pp. 100–01)

· ❀ ·

The Buddha does not look down on living beings from on high. He lifts them up to the same level as himself. He teaches them that they are all equally treasure towers worthy of supreme respect. This is the philosophy of the Lotus Sutra and Nichiren's spirit. It is true humanism. (*Buddhism Day by Day*, p. 292)

· ❀ ·

In an age when both society and the religious world are wrought by turmoil and confusion, only a teaching that gives each individual the power to draw forth his or her innate Buddha nature can lead all people to happiness and transform the tenor of the times. In other words, the only way to realize happiness and peace for people in the Latter Day is by developing our great human potential. There can be no substantial solution to society's problems that does not involve developing our state of life.

When we delve deeper into the idea of relieving people's suffering expounded in the Lotus Sutra, we can see that it is pervaded with a genuine spirit of humanism. Keenly sensing the real nature of the Latter Day of the Law, the Daishonin revealed this humanistic aspect of the Lotus Sutra in his teaching . . .

Buddhist humanism is not grounded in a fixed conceptual framework; it is based on each person's potential to achieve their human revolution by cultivating his or her inherent Buddha nature. (April 2002 *Living Buddhism*, pp. 10–11)

· ❀ ·

The SGI is a world of humanity—of the heart, of faith, of compassion. It is a world of unity and mutual inspiration. That is why it is strong. If we continue to value and promote these qualities, the SGI will continue to grow and develop forever. I want to declare here and now the atmosphere where we can discuss anything is fundamental to the SGI. (*For Today and Tomorrow*, p. 86)

History *of* Buddhist
HUMANISM

*Key Buddhist philosophers and
reformers leading up to the founding
presidents of the SGI*

The HUMANISM of SHAKYAMUNI BUDDHA

Introduction to Series

Buddhism values the innate dignity of all life regardless of gender, age, ethnicity, social standing, wealth or any other factor. The Soka Gakkai International's heritage of faith flows from the teachings of Shakyamuni Buddha and Nichiren Daishonin, based on the vow to help all people transform suffering and misery into absolute, indestructible happiness. Ours is the conviction that Buddhahood—the life-condition of enlightenment—exists in all people and that peace is realized through the compassionate act of awakening people to the Buddha nature within themselves.

Though Shakyamuni wished to elevate the lives of all people without exception, history shows that Buddhism's core beliefs of equality and respect for all were often buried under tradition, formalities and rituals that eclipsed the common people's needs. But Buddhist history also shows that, at various times, reformers appeared on the scene, intent on leading the people back to the Buddha's fundamental purpose: wisdom and unshakable happiness for all.

In this series, *Living Buddhism* will briefly chronicle the development of Buddhism since its founding, and the transmission of its spirit and message of empowering humanism until today. We will look at the contributions of some of the Buddhist Order's key egalitarian philosophers and reformers, leading up to today's SGI.

Shakyamuni's Early Life

Details about Shakyamuni's life are often mixed with folklore and, as such, are difficult to prove. But Buddhist scholars generally agree that Shakyamuni was born roughly 2,500 years ago in Lumbini Gardens, an area near today's India-Nepal border. His father, King Shuddhodana, ruled the Shakya clan, inhabitants of the region. The name *Shakyamuni* means "Sage of the Shakyas." His name at birth is uncertain but is thought to have been Siddhartha Gautama. Shakyamuni's mother, Maya, died soon after giving birth. His maternal aunt, Mahaprajapati (also married to Shuddhodana) raised him.

Brahmans likely tutored the young prince in philosophy, religious epics, law, warfare and statecraft. While in his teens, he married his cousin Yashodhara. In his biography of Shakyamuni, *The*

Members listen to an experience at a Jenkintown District discussion meeting, Abington, Pennsylvania, February 2009.

Jonathan Wilson

Living Buddha, SGI President Ikeda considers what the Buddha must have been like as a youth: "The Shakya state was small and weak and constantly threatened by its neighbors. His keen sensibility and devotion to justice must have kept him pondering day and night some way to lead his people to safety. He was given to meditation and introspection in spite of the warm and inviting surroundings in which he was raised, and this was because he was deeply concerned about the future role of leader that he was destined to play. The youthful Shakyamuni, I believe, can best be described as a humanist and seeker after truth who had a keen sense of justice" (p. 13).

The young Shakyamuni's introspective nature no doubt played a significant part in his choosing to leave the security of the palace in search of life's ultimate truth. What prompted this drastic decision? His observation of the four universal sufferings of birth, aging, sickness and death. According to one explanation: leaving one day through the eastern gate of the palace, he saw an elderly man; on another occasion, departing from the southern gate, he saw a sick person; and exiting yet another time from the western gate, he saw a corpse. These encounters led him to the realization that all who are born will age, will face illness and will eventually die. Lastly, departing from the northern gate, he saw a wandering ascetic whose self-assured and purposeful demeanor impressed him. The story of these four encounters can be considered a metaphor for realizations that came as a result of his significant pondering.

Why do we all suffer in life? What is suffering's purpose? What do we do with our pain, and how can we help others? Shakyamuni became determined to answer these questions.

The Departure and Asceticism

Until his awakening to the four sufferings, Shakyamuni's entire life had been centered on his role as his father's heir. His decision to leave must have been terribly difficult. Not only was he stepping away from his political future, he also had a young son, Rahula (according to some accounts, he had another son, Sunakshatra). King

Shuddhodana pleaded with him not to leave, but Shakyamuni's passion to grasp the real nature of life and death prevailed. And so, he left the palace in search of truth.

At that time, new religious movements were gaining popularity in India. Six prominent teachers led philosophical movements in the northern Indian states. Their teachings were, in general, rejections of the prevailing Brahmanic social order and Vedic teachings. They ranged from a form of hedonism (focusing on the theory that pleasure or satisfaction of desires is the highest good and proper aim of human life) to asceticism (austere practices aimed at severely limiting material pursuits as a means to achieving a transcendent state). Some of these teachings questioned the purpose of morality. Of the six, only one teaching—Jainism—has survived. Shakyamuni no doubt encountered practitioners of these teachings, but none sufficiently answered the mysteries he hoped to unravel.

He studied meditation under two teachers. But after mastering all they had to teach, he left them. He then focused on ascetic practices, which greatly appealed to him and stood in contrast to the lush lifestyle of the palace. For nearly 10 years, Shakyamuni followed a course of incredibly strict asceticism.

President Ikeda writes: "The scriptures record that those around him were astonished by the severity of the practices that he undertook, and at one point even believed that he had died as a result. In his later years, when he was recalling this period of his life, he recollects that no Brahman or *shramana* ascetic in the past had ever undergone—nor would any ever be likely to undergo—the kind of severe self-torture that he himself had endured, although he did not thereby gain enlightenment.

"The note of self-assurance in this statement is important, for it indicates that he was convinced that he had entered into these ascetic practices determinedly and wholeheartedly and had persisted until he had penetrated into the very essence of such practices. When, failing to attain the goal that he sought, he later abandoned such practices, he did so not out of frustration or a failure of willpower but only after he had grasped the quintessence of asceticism and found it of no use to him" (*The Living Buddha*, pp. 48–49).

In other words, Shakyamuni came to realize that while meditation and self-restriction were important tools, neither would lead directly to understanding the sufferings he had observed in life.

Enlightenment

Legend has it that after turning his back on ascetic practices, Shakyamuni went to a river to bathe. He had wasted away to such a degree that he could barely manage to leave the river. After years of intense fasting, his first meal was a bowl of rice boiled in milk, a gift from a young girl. Bathed and fed, he then sat in meditation beneath a pipal (a variety of fig) tree. The effect of many years of self-reflection, coupled with renewed vigor from the bath and food, allowed Shakyamuni to delve into greater depths of meditation than he had ever before reached.

During this episode of intense concentration and insight, the legend continues, Shakyamuni faced Mara, the devil king. Mara, representing fundamental darkness—ignorance or disbelief in one's own enlightened potential—tried to awaken fear and doubt in Shakyamuni, tempting him to worry over his health, his determination and his self-worth.

Ray Marcero speaks at a Jenkintown District discussion meeting.

Jonathan Wilson

"Emaciated and ashen of complexion," Mara told Shakyamuni, "you are on the verge of death. Your chance of survival is one in a thousand. You ought to live, for only when alive it is possible for you to do good deeds . . . However, your present efforts are vain and futile, for the way to the true dharma is hard, painful, and inaccessible" (*The Living Buddha*, pp. 55–56).

But Shakyamuni did not waver. "Friend of the slothful, Evil One," he said to Mara, "you have come here for your own sake . . . Lusts are your first army, the second is called Aversion. Your third army is Hunger and Thirst, the fourth Craving. Your fifth is Sloth and Indolence, the sixth Cowardice. Your seventh army is Doubt, the eighth Hypocrisy and Stupidity. Gain, Fame, Honor, and Glory falsely obtained, the Lauding of oneself and Condemning of others. This is your army, Evil One. The coward does not overcome it, but he who overcomes it attains happiness" (*The Living Buddha*, pp. 56–57).

Shakyamuni's spirit, in fighting his fundamental darkness, is the same spirit to which Nichiren Daishonin referred when writing: "You should not have the slightest fear in your heart. It is lack of courage that prevents one from attaining Buddhahood" ("The Three Obstacles and Four Devils," *The Writings of Nichiren Daishonin*, vol. 1, p. 637).

Shakyamuni, through the power of his resolve, defeated Mara and attained enlightenment. Regarding this auspicious moment, President Ikeda writes: "As the darkness of night began to give way to the first light of dawn, the state of Buddhahood existing in the universe and the state of Buddhahood inherent in Shakyamuni's own life merged in harmonious communion and blossomed forth. Thus, Shakyamuni's enlightenment was a kind of mutual response that took place between these two states of Buddhahood" (*The Living Buddha*, pp. 59–60).

In brief, free of delusion, Shakyamuni perceived the endless life of the universe manifested in the intricate interrelation of all phenomena. He understood in the depths of his being that delusion is the root cause of suffering. Delusion means the seeking of happiness and security in transient phenomena, clinging to things outside us while failing to recognize the eternal nature of life. A person with a deluded mind fails to recognize the universal nobility of human life and, therefore, thinks some people are more worthy than others. In terms of Nichiren Buddhism, this universal and noble aspect of life common to all people is called the Mystic Law, or *myoho*. (For a detailed analysis of Shakyamuni's enlightenment, please see *The Living Buddha*, pp. 53–68.)

Along with Shakyamuni's profound awakening came an endless love and compassion for people. Shakyamuni now saw all people as potential Buddhas who were held back from realizing that potential because of distorted views and ignorance. His enlightenment and compassion became what the Lotus Sutra describes as "a vow, hoping to make all persons equal to me, without any distinction between us" (*The Lotus Sutra and Its Opening and Closing Sutras*, p. 70). Shakyamuni had come to see delusion as a cause of suffering, and he also perceived the means to overcome it. Developing teachings and practices to lead all people to enlightenment and inspiring people to pursue that path became his life's work.

It is said that Shakyamuni, upon dedicating his life to eradicating human suffering and misery, was once again accosted by Mara, who attempted to dissuade him from choosing such a difficult course. Mara's interference signifies that the fundamental darkness innate in life will attempt to hinder one's practice for self and others. Shakyamuni more easily defeated Mara this second time and then, leaving the shade of the fig grove, began his lifelong quest to fulfill his vow.

—*Prepared by* Living Buddhism

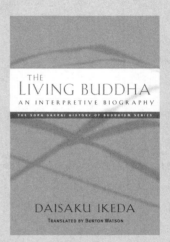

For more on the life of Shakyamuni Buddha, take a look at *The Living Buddha: An Interpretive Biography* by SGI President Daisaku Ikeda.

Visit the Middleway Press website at www.middlewaypress.com or visit your local or online bookseller. ISBN: 978-0-9779245-2-3; $14.95.

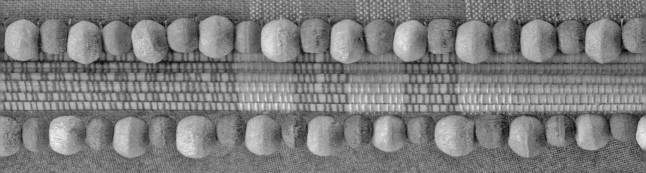

History *of* Buddhist
HUMANISM

*Key Buddhist philosophers and
reformers leading up to the founding
presidents of the SGI*

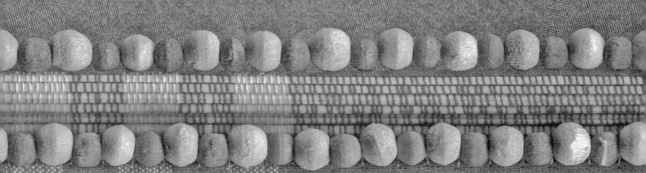

TURNING the WHEEL of the LAW

The journey from Gaya, where Shakyamuni awakened to his enlightened nature, to Deer Park in Sarnath, where he first taught what he had realized, takes about 10 days on foot. Shakyamuni made this journey, rather than begin teaching in Gaya, because he wished first to share his understanding with five wandering ascetics with whom he had studied earlier.

Some scriptures say the five ascetics, who had been critical of Shakyamuni's renunciation of the most austere practices, were not terribly pleased to see him and treated him at first with disdain. But, moved by his dignified demeanor, they eventually warmed to their old friend and listened to what he had to say. This moment is known as the first "turning of the wheel of the Law" and marks the beginning of Buddhism as a philosophical movement.

None of the five immediately became Shakyamuni's disciple, nor did the Buddha push them to do so. He stayed with them for many days, talking to them until one, Kaundinya, and later the other four, determined to follow him.

SGI President Ikeda writes: "It can be said that Buddhism began from a kind of discussion meeting. When Shakyamuni 'began turning the wheel of the Law'—that is, when he first shared the content of his enlightenment with others— he did so not before a large assembly but in the form of a small meeting. He sat down with five old friends and talked with them in an intimate, informal way. They became Shakyamuni's first five disciples. This discussion meeting, in which the ties of mentor and disciple were first forged, is really the start of Buddhism. It was a discussion meeting that marked the dawn of a spiritual revolution that would illuminate humanity— namely, *kosen-rufu*" (January–February 2010 *Living Buddhism*, pp. 10–11).

Thus, the *sangha*, or Buddhist community, was born through friendship and dialogue. Simply meeting with people and discussing life in an open and encouraging manner remained Shakyamuni's principal method of teaching throughout his life.

What, during the first turning of the wheel of the Law, did Shakyamuni teach? President Ikeda encapsulates the first teachings in his interpretive biography of Shakyamuni, *The Living Buddha*:

It is generally asserted that he began by explaining the Middle Way, urging the rejection of both extreme hedonism and extreme asceticism. After he had made his position clear on this point, he proceeded to teach the four noble truths and the eightfold path. There is a great deal of controversy among scholars concerning the reliability of this account, however, some claiming that only the eightfold path was taught, others that the Buddha's initial teachings consisted of the four noble truths, and that the Middle Way and the eightfold path were added much later.

We can only guess as to which theory is correct. It is safe to conjecture, however, that after gaining enlightenment under the bodhi tree, Shakyamuni labored long and conscientiously over the precise form in which he would first present his teachings to the world. To explain the realm of supreme and mysterious wisdom in such a way that it would be comprehensible to others, he had to bring his explanations down to a more popular level and translate the principles of enlightenment into terms that could be generally understood and embraced.

If we accept the hypothesis that what Shakyamuni taught first was the four noble truths, we should note immediately that these represent a very realistic and practical doctrine. They begin by defining the problem, declaring that (1) all existence is suffering and that (2) suffering is caused by selfish craving. They then proceed to present the solution to the problem of suffering, asserting that (3) selfish craving can be destroyed and that (4) it can be destroyed by following the eightfold path.

The eightfold path is likewise an extremely clear and concrete list of principles to be followed in order to gain deliverance—namely, the observance of (1) right views, (2) right thinking, (3) right speech, (4) right action, (5) right way of life, (6) right endeavor, (7) right mindfulness, and (8) right meditation.

Because of the extremely simple and practical nature of these doctrines, the five ascetics were able to understand them with relative ease. It is for the same reason that followers of Mahayana Buddhism regard these early doctrines (along with the Agama sutras that record them) as forms of the Law that have been adapted to the level of understanding of ordinary people and designed to entice them in the direction of an understanding of the higher principles of the Law. That would mean that this first sermon is less an approximation of the essence of Shakyamuni's enlightenment than a simple program for religious practice intended to lead people toward that enlightenment. (*The Living Buddha*, pp. 74–75)

The Growth of the Order

From the day Shakyamuni left the palace where he had grown up as a prince, he never again took up permanent residence. He traveled throughout what is now northern India and Nepal, usually not staying in one place longer than a single season. As he continued to travel and teach, the Buddhist community grew rapidly. His disciples came from all walks of life: from the Kshatriya (warrior) caste or class (including many of his family members), as well as the Brahman (priest) class, merchant classes and Chandala (the lowest caste). In a society as socially regimented as ancient India, where classes could not be crossed, Shakyamuni's acceptance of all people was highly unusual, perhaps even unique at the time.

Preaching the Dharma to all people required patience, creativity and boldness. Degrees of wealth and education, careers and even language varied from class to class. Because of this, Shakyamuni was known to take into account the capacity of the people he addressed and tailor his teaching to best suit their understanding. The incredible variety of Buddhist teachings, when later committed to writing, attests to the diversity of teaching methods Shakyamuni employed.

As Nichiren Daishonin puts it, "One who attempts to propagate the teachings of Buddhism must understand the capacity and basic nature of the persons one is addressing" ("The Teaching, Capacity, Time, and Country," *The Writings of Nichiren Daishonin*, vol. 1, p. 48). Shakyamuni knew that little could be gained by preaching in the same way to all people; some would gain wisdom but others would not, and

Rego Ghorbani

SGI-USA members at the Dallas North Activity Center, October 2009.

still others might turn away from the Dharma if not instructed correctly.

Many of Shakyamuni's best-known disciples came from the Kshatriya caste—as Shakyamuni did—or from the religious Brahman caste, as these were the most likely to be well-educated wandering philosophers. But the sutras include numerous stories of merchant, pauper and tradesperson disciples. Shakyamuni clearly embraced people from all corners of Indian society.

A few of Shakyamuni's principal disciples had been religious or philosophical leaders with disciples of their own before joining the Buddhist Order. Shariputra and Maudgalyayana, childhood friends born in the Brahman caste, were important leaders in a nihilistic movement. Nihilism, however, ultimately dissatisfied them, and after hearing a simple teaching explained by one of Shakyamuni's first five disciples, they became Buddhists, taking with them the majority of members of the nihilistic group they had once led. They became, in time, two of Shakyamuni's most trusted companions.

Ananda, Aniruddha and Devadatta were Shakyamuni's cousins. Shakyamuni's son, former wife and adoptive mother later became disciples as well. While each played an important role in the growth of the Order, there's no indication of favoritism from Shakyamuni for simply being related to him.

Devadatta's Betrayal

As the years passed and the Buddhist community grew, there came to be two essential categories of practitioners: monastic and lay.

The monks traveled with the Buddha, begged for alms, learned, meditated and taught. They led lives of restriction from material pleasures, though far less harsh than Shakyamuni's practices had been before he renounced asceticism.

Lay believers did not usually travel with them, but sought to learn the Buddha's teachings where they lived. They supported the Buddha and the traveling monks through almsgiving.

The relationship between monk and lay believer ideally created a mutually supportive system, but it was not without its own challenges. Sometimes, monks would walk slowly past the houses of the rich but walk quickly through poorer neighborhoods, or they would pay more attention to rich patrons while ignoring the needs of those less wealthy or lower in social standing. And there were lay believers who simply sought to improve their karma through donations without trying to incorporate the teachings of the Buddha in their actions.

The Buddha and his most trusted disciples took direct responsibility for correcting these negative behaviors. As a result, the sutras, especially the Mahayana sutras, contain frequent warnings against favoritism and laziness of any kind, and, most important, they stress the significance of compassion for all and a personal dedication to attaining Buddhahood.

For example, a passage in the Vimalakirti Sutra praises the Buddha's self-reliance, saying, "You have mastered the marks of all phenomena, no blocks or hindrances; like the sky, you lean on nothing."[1] The Lotus Sutra makes frequent mention of people of "overbearing arrogance" claiming to have attained what they have not. It states that leading others to enlightenment is the "one great reason alone" for a Buddha's existence and also says that in order to "put aside all sloth and remissness, one must understand the Lotus Sutra (see *The Lotus Sutra and Its Opening and Closing Sutras*, p. 64, p. 67 and p. 206).

The most glaring and dangerous challenge to the Buddha's teaching during his lifetime came from his cousin Devadatta. Charming, intelligent and seemingly virtuous, Devadatta secretly harbored a deep-seated jealously toward Shakyamuni. He sought to make himself more popular than Shakyamuni, claiming that the Buddha had become old and weak-willed, and needed to be replaced.

Devadatta gained the favor of Prince Ajatashatru, the son of one of Shakyamuni's greatest supporters, King Bimbisara, thereby causing strife within the royal family of Magadha, as well as fomenting a schism in the Buddhist Order. Ajatashatru, goaded by Devadatta, overthrew and imprisoned his father.

Devadatta also concocted various schemes to discredit or injure Shakyamuni.

A recurring theme in Buddhist history is that no matter how virtuous a person appears to be, if their motivation is selfish, they will only cause disunity. Shakyamuni recognized the dangerous egotism in his cousin's actions and publicly reprimanded Devadatta for his arrogance.

Devadatta left the Buddhist Order, taking with him 500 or so supporters. Shakyamuni immediately sent Shariputra and Maudgalyayana to meet with Devadatta's followers. It is said that the two were so successful in bringing these dissenters back into the Order that Devadatta coughed up blood in rage.

The historical Devadatta became a symbolic figure in later Buddhist writings representing the destructive and arrogant potential in all people. In the Lotus Sutra, a chapter is dedicated to him, illustrating that the Buddha nature exists in all people, even the least virtuous. As Nichiren says, "Devadatta also represents the principle that our earthly desires are none other than enlightenment" (*The Record of the Orally Transmitted Teachings*, p. 107).

Women in the Buddhist Order

At its inception, the Buddhist Order only admitted men. Scholars have long debated why this was so, given Shakyamuni's well-established disregard for caste and social standing. One reason may be that he feared men would be distracted from monastic discipline by the presence of women.

President Ikeda writes: "He was anxious that his followers, once they had become monks, should reach the same high level of enlightenment that he himself had attained, but he knew that this required great effort and concentration. The monks had renounced secular life and set out upon the path toward higher understanding. For this reason, they had to be sheltered from any influence that might frustrate their efforts and deflect them from their course. It was with concerns of this kind, I believe, that Shakyamuni hesitated for so long to admit women to the Order" (*The Living Buddha*, p. 118).

As the Order grew and traveled, an increasing number of women requested to be part of it. Ananda, who served as a sort of personal assistant to Shakyamuni, is said to have frequently requested that women be allowed to join the Order. Shakyamuni eventually agreed, and Mahaprajapati—his aunt and adoptive mother—became the first *bhikkhuni*, or Buddhist nun.

In the Lotus Sutra, the four kinds of believers—monks, nuns, laymen and laywomen—are repeatedly presented as equals.

Shakyamuni's Death

Shakyamuni had always placed tremendous trust in his disciples Maudgalyayana and Shariputra, and if any of the disciples were meant to lead the *sangha* after his death, they seemed the likeliest candidates. It is possible, however, that no single leader was ever intended to succeed him. According to President Ikeda, Shakyamuni seems to have considered himself a member of the Buddhist Order more than its leader (see *The Living Buddha*, p. 131).

In any event, Shariputra and Maudgalyayana died before Shakyamuni—Shariputra of illness, and Maudgalyayana murdered by a jealous Brahman. Their deaths, which occurred in rapid succession, caused considerable heartache for Shakyamuni. Still, he did not allow even this heavy blow to disrupt his ongoing teaching and traveling.

Toward the end of his life, Shakyamuni spent a while at Gridhrakuta, better known as Eagle Peak, where he is said to have taught the Lotus Sutra. After this, when he was around 80, he journeyed to Vaishali in present-day northwestern Bihar, where he contracted what appears to have been dysentery. Shakyamuni died in a grove of sal trees, which, according to legend, burst into full bloom at the moment of his death and showered his body with flowers.

The Mahaparinirvana Sutra, which focuses on the six months before and after Shakyamuni's death, records many moments of instruction regarding how the community of believers should be managed after his death. For example, he tells Ananda: "Therefore, you must be your own islands. Take the self as your refuge. Take refuge in nothing outside yourselves. Hold firm to the Law as an island, and do not seek refuge in anything besides yourselves" (*The Living Buddha*, p. 132).

Regarding this passage, President Ikeda writes:

> One tends to think of the self as rather frail and unreliable, and it may seem surprising to find the Buddha laying such emphasis upon it. By "self" here, however, he does not mean the ordinary self that is subject to sudden changes through the influence of outside causes but the self that aspires to a state of permanence through the Law. Once such a self is firmly established, then one of the fundamental objectives of Buddhism has been realized and the individual is free to devote the remainder of his or her time to the salvation of others and the perpetuation of the Law.
>
> In Buddhism, dependence on others is not sought, and help from others is not awaited. The individual must establish a sound understanding, bright and clear as a mirror, and march forward solely accompanied by that understanding. The Law is the foundation upon which to build such a self. And the Law is inherent within the life of each and every individual; it does not exist outside the self. (*The Living Buddha*, p. 132)

After the Buddha's death, Ananda and other disciples met to determine how best to continue and promote the growth of the *sangha*.

—*Prepared by* Living Buddhism

1. *The Vimalakirti Sutra*, translated by Burton Watson (New York: Columbia University Press, 1997), p. 25.

History *of* Buddhist
HUMANISM

*Key Buddhist philosophers and
reformers leading up to the founding
presidents of the SGI*

The DEVELOPMENT of MAHAYANA BUDDHISM

According to accounts of the time shortly after Shakyamuni Buddha's death, his close disciple Mahakashyapa stated: "Friends, we must make certain that the teachings and ordinances are put into proper form, rendering it impossible for false doctrines to flourish while true ones decline, for false ordinances to be set up while true ones are discarded, for expounders of false teachings to grow strong while expounders of the truth grow weak, for expounders of false ordinances to seize power while expounders of true ones lose it" (*Buddhism, the First Millennium*, p. 3).

With this protective desire in mind, 500 monks gathered to discuss the future of the Buddhist Order. They met under the patronage of King Ajatashatru, a former disciple of Devadatta and former enemy of Buddhism. Toward the end of the Buddha's life, the king changed dramatically and converted to Buddhism.

Led by senior disciples such as Ananda, Mahakashyapa and Upali, the 500 monks decided to make the teachings their leader, as Shakyamuni had advised them to do, rather than appointing an individual to lead the Order.

Ananda, who had served as personal assistant to his cousin Shakyamuni, had witnessed a great many of the Buddha's discussions and sermons. Ananda is also said to have possessed an astounding memory. The traditional opening line of sutras "This is what I heard" specifically refers to Ananda. The *I* in the phrase can also be interpreted to mean the Buddhist practitioner reciting the sutra as a declaration of faith in the teaching it contained (see *The Record of the Orally Transmitted Teachings*, pp. 9–10).

The Buddhist teachings recounted by Ananda were not written down but committed to memory through recitation and were meant to be put into practice in daily life. Because of this, sutra recitation and very strict keeping of precepts became central to the lives of the monks after the First Buddhist Council, as this initial gathering came to be known.

While the First Council constituted the largest organized effort to preserve Shakyamuni's teachings, his disciples were not in universal agreement with the teachings and disciplines the Council created.

Some, especially among the laity, were not in attendance. Some monks peacefully disagreed and parted with the First Council. This was the case with Purna, for example, who "intended to carry out the teachings of the Buddha in accordance with the way he himself had heard them expounded by Shakyamuni" (*Buddhism, the First Millennium*, p. 12).

SGI President Ikeda notes: "In the historical growth of Buddhism in this early period, it was the canon fixed by the First Council, regarded with the utmost reverence and gravity, that served as the core of faith. And, although that canon may have had its imperfections and deficiencies, the determination of the people who compiled it to ensure the continuance of the dharma was the factor that led in time to the birth of the whole great corpus of Buddhist teachings" (*Buddhism, the First Millennium*, p. 13).

After roughly 100 years, monks from the city of Vriji asked for a new interpretation of certain rules of monastic discipline they felt were too stringent and did not fit their circumstances.

Seven hundred monks assembled to discuss and resolve the matter, and this gathering came to be known as the Second Buddhist Council.

The Second Council flatly rejected the suggested rule changes, and this eventually led to a schism in the order. The faction made up of the more conservative adherents of the rules of discipline later became known as Theravada, or the Teaching of the Elders, and the progressive group became known as Mahasamghika, or Members of the Great Order. Further schisms occurred, and within another hundred years, at least 17 schools had formed around various interpretations of discipline, doctrine and the role of the laity.

The Transformation of King Ashoka

Some 250 years after Shakyamuni, a violent and tyrannical ruler named Ashoka, of the central Asian Mauryan dynasty, converted to Buddhism. It seems not to have had a great effect on him at first: Even after his conversion, he launched his bloodiest war against the state of Kalinga, in which it is said 100,000 people died.

By the end of this war, however, the Buddhist teachings had penetrated his life, and the sufferings of war made him grieve terribly. He vowed to rule based on the Buddhist Law and not by force, and he never went to war again.

During his reign as king of nearly all of India, he went from being known as "Ashoka the tyrant" to "Ashoka of the Dharma." Among his many works, he established state health and veterinary care, had fruit trees planted and wells dug along trade routes, forbade animal sacrifice, declared religious freedom and created a government office to address the needs of women.

Ashoka did not merely tolerate non-Buddhist religious groups. He donated food and land to them, as he felt they deserved respect and freedom. He also gave alms to Buddhist schools and made pilgrimages to Buddhist sites. Instead of partaking in the sort of vacations traditionally enjoyed by royalty, he made excursions to teach the principles of Buddhism. He is said to have commissioned construction of thousands of stupas and temples. During Ashoka's lifetime, Buddhism flourished among monks and laity.

The Great Vehicle

About five centuries after Shakyamuni's death, sutras and sutra commentaries became increasingly committed to writing. This allowed for teachings to spread with improved consistency and greater effect among the laity, who could not reasonably dedicate many hours each day to sutra recitation.

Though the First Council intended to create standards of Buddhist orthodoxy, it did not necessarily consider the needs of the lay believers or the teachings aimed at them. It was a monastic order and recorded monastic teachings, primarily focused on living a life of great discipline and eradicating desire.

The Mauryan dynasty faded a few generations after Ashoka, and the dynasty that followed it was antagonistic toward Buddhism. Many Buddhist schools faltered in this climate. Schools further split as sectarian debate and fear of persecution

Thomas Chan

Youth practice a song at a Rock the Era activity, SGI-USA San Francisco Culture Center, November 2009.

threatened to override Buddhism's courageous and compassionate essence. In this climate of decline, a Buddhist reformation movement arose: Mahayana, or "Great Vehicle."

Far from an organized movement, the early Mahayana grew in scattered pockets throughout northern India. It spread rapidly, however, through the enthusiasm of its practitioners.

President Ikeda notes: "The Mahayana movement that sprang up in many regions of India at this time may be seen as an attempt to reform Buddhism and reverse its decline, partly by combating the factionalism and strife that had come to characterize the Buddhist Order in its traditional form. It was a Buddhist equivalent of the Reformation in Europe, a movement to restore vitality to the faith. That the Buddhist Order faced the danger of political antagonism or outright persecution only served to strengthen in the leaders of the Mahayana movement their consciousness of themselves as Buddhists and their determination to fight for their beliefs" (*Buddhism, the First Millennium*, p. 79).

The Mahayanists referred to Theravada and other older schools as "Hinayana," the "Lesser Vehicle." Mahayana teachings differed from Theravada in many ways. Mahayana schools sought a return to Shakyamuni's spirit to help all people instead of focusing on the monastic orders and rules of discipline. Theravada practice aimed at attaining the state of *arhat*, a sage who is free from rebirth. The bodhisattva ideal and practice, however, became central to the Mahayana teachings, which taught that the Buddha nature is inherent in all life. Also, the Mahayana teachings, while not exclusively lay-oriented, placed far greater emphasis on the laity and on spreading the teachings than did Theravada.

The Lotus Sutra

The single most important Mahayana scripture is the Lotus Sutra. Mahayana tradition holds that Shakyamuni, toward the end of his life, taught the Lotus Sutra over an eight-year period, and the sermons were passed down and later compiled as *Saddharma-pundarika-sutra,* or the Lotus Sutra of the Wonderful Law.

Given that the Theravada teachings were the product of monks dedicated to preserving the Buddha's teachings, while the Lotus Sutra and other Mahayana writings appeared without such a clearly established lineage, some have questioned the authenticity of the Lotus Sutra and other Mahayana scriptures. It should be remembered, however, that the laity was not the focus of the First Council, nor were all the Buddha's teachings included in the Theravada canon.[1]

President Ikeda, examining the question of whether lay Buddhist organizations existed distinct from, and contemporaneous with, Theravada, writes: "I am strongly inclined to think that such an organization did exist, though we must await further study before we can attempt to say just what form it had. The Vimalakirti Sutra centers around an enlightened and highly influential lay believer named Vimalakirti. Some scholars would view him as a purely fictitious figure, an embodiment of the ideal layperson, but I wonder if he did not have real-life models among the outstanding lay leaders of the early Buddhist community. And I wonder if the Vimalakirti Sutra and works like it are not in fact the product of some formal group or religious organization, though not one as tightly knit as the Buddhist Order itself.

"The Lotus Sutra as well would seem to have been transmitted by an organization of enlightened laity" (*Buddhism, the First Millennium,* pp. 92–93).

Nagarjuna's Impact on the Development of Buddhism

While the Mahayana movement involved monks and laity throughout India (mostly in the north), one significant philosopher stands out. Nagarjuna, who lived seven centuries after the

Buddha, was a southern Indian Brahman who converted to Buddhism as a youth. He is widely regarded as the most influential Indian Buddhist thinker after Shakyamuni himself. In fact, he is sometimes referred to as "the second Buddha." The Great Teacher Tiantai[2] and Nichiren Daishonin both held Nagarjuna in very high esteem.

He is said to have read through the sutras, rules of discipline and commentaries in 90 days. Still unsatisfied, he set out to learn more, and in his travels studied the Mahayana teachings and, eventually, the Lotus Sutra. The Mahayana movement was still fairly scattered, and Nagarjuna spent almost half his life traveling from one Mahayana school to the next, reading, discussing and comparing teachings of the schools he had encountered. Wherever he went, Nagarjuna debated with Buddhists and non-Buddhists, and helped to systematize and codify the Mahayana teachings, which led to a fortified movement, one with a stronger sense of unity and drive. Without his efforts, Mahayana might never have become so widely practiced.

Nagarjuna was an incredibly prolific author, whose contributions to Buddhist thought are difficult to enumerate. Most significant is his investigation of Shakyamuni's doctrinal core. Nagarjuna wished to convey the essential nature of the Buddha's way of understanding phenomena, which he characterized as non-dualistic.

From this, he derived the concepts of non-substantiality (Skt *shunyata,* often translated as "emptiness" or "void") and the Middle Way (Skt *madhyama-pratipad*). The concept of "changing poison into medicine," a familiar concept for many SGI members, also comes from Nagarjuna.

Providing a concise statement on non-dualism, Nichiren writes: "Life is indeed an elusive reality that transcends both the words and concepts of existence and nonexistence. It is neither existence nor nonexistence, yet exhibits the qualities of both" ("On Attaining Buddhahood in This Lifetime," *The Writings of Nichiren Daishonin,* vol. 1, p. 4).

Since the complex interactions of phenomena cannot be pointed to directly, Nagarjuna relied

Rob Nevitt

Youth in Seattle prepare for their performance
in the annual Seafair Parade, July 2009.

on a series of negations to derive a sense of life's mysterious nature.

President Ikeda writes: "It is through this process of negation of every possible concept that one arrives at an understanding of the *shunyata,* or non-substantiality, that is the core of Nagarjuna's philosophy of the Middle Way.

"It is important to note, however, that the non-substantiality we arrive at through this process of negation is not the same as mere 'nothingness.' It is described as 'empty' or 'void' because we have negated all the possible characteristics or predicates that might ordinarily be used to describe it, but it is totally different in its essential nature from the kind of nothingness that is customarily associated with nihilistic thought. Such a mere nothingness or non-being, which is the opposite of being, would of course in Nagarjuna's thought be negated along with all other concepts. The true non-substantiality of the Middle Way is therefore a nothingness that transcends both non-being and being.

"Nothing can be born out of mere nothingness. But from the non-substantiality of the Middle Way, which is a kind of infinite potentiality, anything and everything may be born or produced, depending upon what causes happen to affect it. Various objects and phenomena appear to the ordinary beholder to be arising out of nothing. But what precedes them is not in fact nothingness but the state of potentiality that Nagarjuna has been describing" (*Buddhism, the First Millennium*, pp. 147–48).

Though philosophically challenging and dense with meaning, Nagarjuna's doctrine of the Middle Way influenced nearly every Buddhist school that came after him, especially those in China and Japan. And it was in those countries, through the teachings of Tiantai and Nichiren, that the doctrine of the Middle Way—ultimately a means to approach the essence of the Lotus Sutra—would be expanded upon and revitalized.

—*Prepared by* Living Buddhism

1. For a more detailed analysis, see *Buddhism, the First Millennium*, pp. 113–37.

2. Tiantai: *The Flower of Chinese Buddhism* uses the Pinyin method of Chinese transliteration. Tiantai is the Pinyin spelling whereas T'ien-t'ai is of the older Wade-Giles method.

History *of* **Buddhist**
HUMANISM

*Key Buddhist philosophers and
reformers leading up to the founding
presidents of the SGI*

The SPREAD of BUDDHISM in CHINA

Shakyamuni Buddha's compassionate vision was never fixed on India alone. The Buddha's teachings are meant to emancipate all people from suffering, and the language of the sutras reflects this. The sutras refer to the Buddha as a teacher of all living beings, a world-honored one, working for the good of all. The Lotus Sutra states: "The buddhas, the world-honored ones, wish to open the door of buddha wisdom to all living beings, to allow them to attain purity. That is why they appear in the world" (*The Lotus Sutra and Its Opening and Closing Sutras*, p. 64).

For centuries after Shakyamuni died, the Theravada school remained strong in southern India and what is now Sri Lanka while the Mahayana schools became increasingly popular in the northern part of the country. These Mahayana schools spread further northward, into central Asia and then China, primarily along the Silk Road, a long, hazardous trade route.

It is not known exactly when Buddhism was introduced to China. Its spread during the reign of King Ashoka[1] is a strong, though unproven, possibility. In any event, it did not become an established presence in China until much later.

Around 67 BCE, Emperor Ming of the Later Han Dynasty is said to have dreamed of a very tall golden man flying in the air. His ministers advised him that the golden man was the Buddha. He then sent envoys to seek out Buddhist missionaries. Two were found in Northern India. A white horse was loaded with sutras and Buddha statues, and the party traveled back to the Han capital of Luoyang and established what came to be known as White Horse Temple.

Whether that story is true or not, historians consider Buddhism's growth in China to be the result of centuries of Mahayana missionaries traveling from India and Central Asia. And the story of Emperor Ming and other stories from that time indicate that Buddhism was a presence in China about 500 years after Shakyamuni, and it seems to have enjoyed favorable relations with the Imperial court in the beginning.

Translating the Sutras

Native schools of thought—Taoism and Confucianism—dominated the scholarly, political, religious and philosophical atmosphere of Chinese life. When Buddhism arrived, the translation of Sanskrit to Chinese had not been established, and there were no formal schools of translation.

The first Buddhists in China—called "barbarian monks" by the Chinese—likely communicated through gestures and a few words, which could not have properly conveyed Buddhism's philosophical scope. Translation of doctrinal materials was of immediate and crucial importance. Chinese scholars, well versed in Confucian doctrine but mostly ignorant of Buddhism, could not reasonably have been expected to take on this task; it fell to the Buddhist monks themselves.

Many early Buddhist translators lived in Central and Western Asia, areas with the greatest Indian-Chinese cultural mixture. Kumarajiva, widely considered the greatest of these translators, was Indian and Kuchan (possibly Uyghur). His father, a monk from what is now Kashmir, became an advisor to the King of Kucha (today part of Xinjiang, China). Kumarajiva's mother was the king's sister.

"Kumarajiva was thus the offspring of an international marriage," notes SGI President Ikeda, "and brought up in a state that played an important role in cultural exchanges between eastern and western Asia" (*The Flower of Chinese Buddhism*, p. 33).

Kumarajiva seems to have been a gifted child. He entered the Buddhist order at 6 or 7 years old and is said to have memorized the equivalent of 32,000 words a day. He not only studied Buddhism but also non-Buddhist Indian philosophy, as well as Taoism and Confucianism. He spent years learning, debating and traveling before focusing on translation.

He lived during a time of political upheaval and warfare. Around 382, Kumarajiva's homeland of Kucha was conquered by forces of the Former Qin dynasty. Although he eventually became an advisor to the conquerors, Kumarajiva remained as little more than a political prisoner.

While enduring repeated indignities, he continued to learn. President Ikeda notes that this period "gave him a chance to mingle with the rough soldiers and other inhabitants of the border region and to see something of the lower side of Chinese life. Most of the monk-translators who had come to China in the past had been men of highly distinguished position who were welcomed by the rulers and aristocracy of China or the members of the intellectual class, and unlike Kumarajiva had little opportunity to become acquainted with other levels of Chinese society" (*The Flower of Chinese Buddhism*, p. 42). This exposure to the common classes may have given Kumarajiva a better understanding of Mahayana's emphasis on the enlightenment of all people.

The Former Qin dynasty fell, and in 401, after more than 16 years in semi-captivity, Kumarajiva traveled to Chang'an. He began work immediately, completing a Buddhist translation in as little as six days after arriving. His first major translation undertaking was *The Treatise on the Great Perfection of Wisdom*, a study of bodhisattva practice attributed to Nagarjuna.

Elsewhere in China, Buddhist monks endured persecution, but in Chang'an, Kumarajiva enjoyed royal patronage and protection, and could therefore pay full attention to his work. In 10 years, Kumarajiva is said to have translated 35 works comprising 294 volumes. Rather than rely on his own knowledge, he would frequently consult other translators and would present his translations to a body of monks who thoroughly scrutinized his work.

He trained hundreds, possibly thousands, of monks in translation and in Buddhist practice. It should be noted, also, that his intent in translating was not merely intellectual passion but rather to propagate the Dharma, saying that he wished to create translations that could "be relied upon for a thousand years to come" (*The Flower of Chinese Buddhism*, pp. 47–48).

His translation of the Lotus Sutra stands out as his most significant achievement. Though not the first Sanskrit-to-Chinese Lotus Sutra translation, Kumarajiva's became the standard and is, to this day, revered as perhaps the greatest sutra translation of all time.

Nichiren Daishonin had complete confidence in Kumarajiva's work. He writes: "When both old and new translations are taken into consideration, we find that there are 186 persons

Sidney Bell

Youth perform at a Rock the Era meeting in Chicago, November 2009.

who have brought sutras and treatises from India and introduced them to China in translation. With the exception of one man, the Tripitaka Master Kumarajiva, all of these translators have made errors of some kind" ("The Selection of the Time," *The Writings of Nichiren Daishonin*, vol. 1, p. 554). He also wrote, "Kumarajiva alone passed along the sutra texts of Shakyamuni, the lord of teachings, just as they were without adding any private opinions of his own" ("On Attaining Buddhahood in One's Present Form," WND-2, 587).

Formation of the Chinese Schools

With sutras and sutra commentaries reliably translated into Chinese, Buddhism spread quicker than ever but still faced many challenges.

When explaining Buddhist doctrine to people unfamiliar with it, at first, it may seem correct to look for commonalities and conceptual analogies between Buddhism and the native belief systems. But this approach only reveals superficial similarity. For example, the fundamental Buddhist concept of non-substantiality[2] may seem similar to the Taoist idea of emptiness. But closer examination shows that the Buddhist concept refers to the interrelatedness of phenomena while the Taoist concept refers to an unhindered or undirected state of mind.

Much as the religious lexicon of English is steeped in Abrahamic traditions, Chinese religious vocabulary was fundamentally Taoist and Confucian. Translation into Chinese, therefore, could not entirely avoid such terminology; it had to be done artfully, so that the Buddhist meaning came through even when using Taoist or Confucian words. Kumarajiva's excellent translations succeeded in this, but understanding the differences and similarities among Buddhist, Taoist and Confucian thought remained a challenge.

Beyond that, Chinese practitioners also had to make sense of the vast variety of Buddhist teachings from India, many of which seemed to contradict one another. This gave rise to many questions. How does one rank sutras? Which sutra and which period of teaching are the most profound? What is the correct practice for attaining enlightenment? Centuries of intense debate surround these questions, from which arose many new Chinese Buddhist traditions and schools of thought.

"We should not, however, think of these divisions as firmly established schools with their own distinctive creeds and practices such as were to come into existence in later centuries of Chinese Buddhism," President Ikeda writes. "Rather, they were individuals or small groups of individuals who, having groped about in the vast literature of Buddhism in an attempt to discover the most apt expression of the Buddha's fundamental teachings, had fixed upon one particular text or system of beliefs as worthy of the highest reverence" (*The Flower of Chinese Buddhism*, p. 58).

Kumarajiva's disciples played decisive roles in systematizing the doctrines. One disciple, Sengrui, was among the first in China to declare the Lotus Sutra superior to all other sutras. Another disciple, Daosheng, publicly declared—to considerable opposition—that all people, including those of incorrigible disbelief, can attain enlightenment.

Origins of the Tiantai[3] School

Toward the end of the fifth century, a monk named Huiwen[4] developed a meditation discipline based on Nagarjuna's doctrines called the "threefold contemplation in a single mind." He created this as a means to observe the non-dual nature of the three truths[5]: non-substantiality, temporary existence and the Middle Way. He transferred his teachings to his disciple Huisi,[6] a diligent and intelligent monk who vowed to master Buddhism after seeing people die and realizing the transitory nature of life.

During Huisi's childhood, the Northern Wei dynasty faltered and split into two states.

President Ikeda writes: "Huisi must have witnessed many scenes of bloodshed and misery during these troubled times. His response to the suffering around him was to set out in search of

the Way so that he might dispel the ignorance of the men and women of his time and lead them to emancipation. In Buddhism, one does not embark on the search for truth merely so that one may accomplish one's own emancipation and satisfy one's own longings for spiritual peace" (*The Flower of Chinese Buddhism*, p. 85).

Buddhism had entered a very intellectual phase in China, with great emphasis placed on scholarship. Huisi, however, took a more active approach and, while studying text, also learned meditation methods and sutra recitation. He became a disciple of Huiwen and, after years of intense faith, practice and study, gained profound insight into the Lotus Sutra. From this, Huisi developed a practice in which the meaning of the sutra is approached through study and recitation, and through deep contemplation.

Huisi's direct disciple, Tiantai Zhiyi[7] (also known as T'ien-t'ai or Chih-i), further developed Lotus Sutra meditation and significantly influenced Chinese Buddhist thought.

The Life of Tiantai Zhiyi

Born near Lake Dongting in southern China around 538, Zhiyi was the son of a government official. His lifelong fascination with the Lotus Sutra and his immense intelligence are well documented. He first encountered the Lotus Sutra at about age 6. After hearing monks reciting the sutra's 25th chapter, "Bodhisattva Perceiver of the World's Sounds," according to some biographies, he memorized it immediately.

Zhiyi received the education befitting the son of a government official, but rather than follow his father's profession, at 18, he became a monk. He focused his attention on the Lotus Sutra almost immediately, which led him to seek out Huisi as his teacher. Huisi, upon meeting Zhiyi, reportedly said: "Long ago we were together on Eagle Peak and listened to the Lotus Sutra. Now, pursuing these old bonds of karma, you have come again" (*The Flower of Chinese Buddhism*, p. 103).

Zhiyi gained profound understanding through Huisi's intense instruction. Before long,

Corey Spicer

Members celebrate February, SGI-USA women's month, in Atlanta, January 31, 2010.

Huisi considered Zhiyi his equal, and Zhiyi left to teach elsewhere.

Zhiyi traveled, taught and studied, undergoing several other periods of awakening to the Dharma. All of this led him to profoundly understand the Lotus Sutra and share his wisdom. He was a prolific lecturer, whose three most important collected works are *The Words and Phrases of the Lotus Sutra*, *The Profound Meaning of the Lotus Sutra* and *Great Concentration and Insight*.[8]

In *Words and Phrases of the Lotus Sutra*, he presents an in-depth 10-volume analysis of the organization and exposition of themes in Kumarajiva's translation. Regarding this, Nichiren Daishonin writes that Zhiyi "explains the various words and phrases in the Lotus Sutra, from the opening words 'This is what I heard' to the final words 'they bowed in obeisance and departed.' He explains them in terms of four categories, namely, causes and conditions, correlated teachings, the theoretical and essential teachings, and the observation of the mind" ("Conversation between a Sage and an Unenlightened Man," WND-1, 133).

The *Profound Meaning of the Lotus Sutra* expresses Zhiyi's enlightenment to the fact of the Lotus Sutra's entire meaning being contained in its title.

Great Concentration and Insight, according to Nichiren, "expounds the meditation on the region of the unfathomable, namely, on the three thousand realms in a single moment of life, based on his thorough understanding of the Lotus Sutra. This is a practice that derives from the Buddha's original enlightenment and represents a principle of truth inherent in one's being" ("Conversation between a Sage and an Unenlightened Man," WND-1, 134).

Tiantai Zhiyi's works and the teachings of Nagarjuna, Huiwen and Huisi formed the doctrines of the Tiantai school.

Three Thousand Realms in a Single Moment of Life

In *The Flower of Chinese Buddhism*, President Ikeda notes that the most important philosophical concept set forth in *Great Concentration and Insight* is that of "three thousand realms in a single moment of life."

He writes: "This concept, which Zhiyi evolved on the basis of teachings in the Lotus Sutra, represents an attempt to explain the mutually inclusive relationship of the ultimate truth and the phenomenal world, of the absolute and the relative" (*The Flower of Chinese Buddhism*, p. 115).

The Ten Worlds are described in earlier Buddhist thought as 10 realms into which beings may be reborn depending upon karma accumulated in past existences. The lowest states of being are hell, hungry spirits, animals and *asuras* (or anger), followed by the worlds of human beings, heavenly beings, voice-hearers and cause-awakened ones; the highest states are bodhisattvas and Buddhas. These states had been viewed as mutually exclusive; in other words, beings occupied one state for an entire lifetime and moved to another state at the beginning of their next lifetime.

President Ikeda elucidates: "In Zhiyi's system of thought, the Ten Worlds are multiplied by various factors that condition them to produce a total of three thousand possible worlds, that is, three thousand realms according to which life may manifest itself. Zhiyi then goes on to state that all of these three thousand possible worlds are present within each instant or 'moment of life' of the individual.

"Within a single lifetime, the individual is capable of moving back and forth any number of times from one realm to another. Thus, one may move upward through religious practice and striving until reaching the ultimate goal, the state of Buddhahood, without going through a lengthy series of rebirths. Or, conversely, the individual may, because of evil deeds or neglect of spiritual concerns, move downward in the scale toward the lower realms of existence" (*The Flower of Chinese Buddhism*, pp. 115–16).

Zhiyi's concept of three thousand realms in a single moment of life explains why in this present lifetime it is possible to attain Buddhahood without having to undergo austere practices over numerous existences, as earlier Buddhist thought asserted. In addition, it also means that even if one attains the state of Buddhahood once, it is not a permanent condition. One must consistently challenge oneself in order to sustain this highest state of life.

Chinese Buddhism and Laity

Various aristocracies ruled China in Zhiyi's time and after, creating a very fertile ground for philosophical development. Buddhism's primary benefactors were the wealthiest and most highly educated members of society. For the most part, it was not a popular movement that easily crossed class boundaries.

Shakyamuni's vow to lead all people to enlightenment—the vow central to the Lotus Sutra—had not changed, however. This vow, unconcerned with wealth, education or social class, is the essence of Mahayana Buddhism. The means to bring it to fruition commenced with the historical Buddha, grew throughout India and became systematized in China. Not until the 13th century in Japan, however, through the efforts of Nichiren Daishonin, was its full potential realized.

—Prepared by Living Buddhism

1. King Ashoka (268–32 BCE): The first king to unify India, who ruled at first as a tyrant but later converted to Buddhism and governed compassionately in accordance with Buddhist ideals. Though devoted to the spread of Buddhism, Ashoka did not enforce it as a state religion. He protected the religious freedom of other religious groups. Ashoka's achievements and views are recorded not only in Buddhist scriptures but also in the many edicts inscribed on rock surfaces and pillars that have been discovered.
2. Non-substantiality (Skt *shunyata*) is the concept that phenomena have no fixed or independent nature of their own. See *The Soka Gakkai Dictionary of Buddhism*, pp. 463–64.
3. Tiantai: *The Flower of Chinese Buddhism* uses the Pinyin method of Chinese transliteration. Tiantai is the Pinyin spelling whereas T'ien-t'ai is of the older Wade-Giles method.
4. Huiwen: Hui-wen in Wade-Giles.
5. The three truths: Also threefold truth, triple truth or three perceptions of the truth. The truth of non-substantiality means that phenomena have no existence of their own; their true nature is non-substantial, indefinable in terms of existence or nonexistence. The truth of temporary existence means that, although non-substantial, all things possess a temporary reality that is in constant flux. The truth of the Middle Way is the essence of things that continues either in a manifest or latent state. The perfect teaching views the three as an integral whole, each possessing all three within itself.
6. Huisi: Also known as Nanyue, or Nan-yueh in Wade-Giles.
7. Zhiyi: Chih-i in Wade-Giles.
8. *The Words and Phrases of the Lotus Sutra*, *The Profound Meaning of the Lotus Sutra* and *Great Concentration and Insight*: For greater detail on these three works, see *The Flower of Chinese Buddhism*, pp. 106–17.

ENLIGHTENED HISTORY

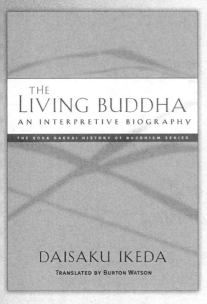

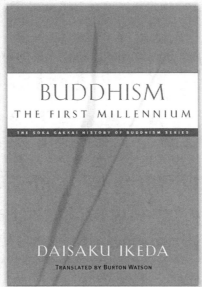

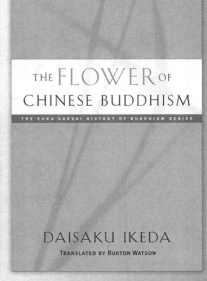

The Living Buddha
goes beyond traditional
biographies of Shakyamuni.
ISBN 978-0-9779245-2-3 · US $14.95

Buddhism, the First Millennium
casts a new light on little-known aspects
of Buddhist history and their relevance to
the understanding of Buddhism today.
ISBN 978-0-9779245-3-0 · US $14.95

The Flower of Chinese Buddhism
illuminates the role of Buddhism
in Chinese society.
ISBN 978-0-9779245-4-7 · US $14.95

Must-reads for any serious student of Buddhism.

**From one of the leading interpreters of Buddhism today, these books give
practical insight into the origins and essence of Mahayana Buddhism.**

Daisaku Ikeda, a spiritual leader for millions, is founding president of the Soka Gakkai International, the world's
largest lay Buddhist organization. **Burton Watson** is a leading translator of Chinese and Japanese literature.

Buddhism For Today

Available at your favorite neighborhood bookstore
or visit middlewaypress.com

History *of* Buddhist
HUMANISM

*Key Buddhist philosophers and
reformers leading up to the founding
presidents of the SGI*

The ESTABLISHMENT of NICHIREN BUDDHISM in JAPAN

The spirit of humanism in Buddhism comes from Shakyamuni Buddha's understanding of life's preciousness and suffering. Shakyamuni's vow, and the fundamental mission of Buddhism, is to lead all people to enlightenment.

As SGI President Ikeda has repeatedly stressed, such humanistic ideals, while at the core of Buddhist philosophy, have not been consistently maintained throughout history but rather have arisen and declined, again and again. The vow to make all people equal to the Buddha stands in contrast to the tendency to see a division between the Buddha and the common mortal.

Nichiren Daishonin took up the Buddha's vow, drawing upon the profound interpretations of Nagarjuna[1] and Tiantai Zhiyi[2] to conceive a practice available to all people. This installment focuses on the events after Zhiyi, leading up to Nichiren.

The Tiantai School After Zhiyi

During the Tang dynasty[3]—a period of economic and artistic prosperity—Buddhism had become a popular and influential aspect of Chinese culture. The dynasty leaders—who traced their lineage to Laozi[4]—opposed the spread of Buddhism and tried to tighten control over it. They feared it would become more popular than Taoism.

Tang emperor Xuanzong established many state-controlled Buddhist temples as a means to control the religion's growth while appearing on the surface to support it.

Miaole Zhanran,[5] the sixth patriarch of the Tiantai school,[6] was summoned to appear before three emperors over the years, but in all cases declined the summons, stating health problems. Because Zhanran traveled long distances throughout his life undeterred by illness, historians have speculated that his refusal was actually because of his distrust and dislike of the Tang dynasty's attempts to control and suppress Buddhism.

As a Confucian scholar turned Buddhist monk, Zhanran became patriarch of the Tiantai school at a time when, despite previous widespread influence, it had fallen into decline. Other schools, such as Chan,[7] Dharma Characteristics[8] and the Flower Garland,[9] became more popular. Imperial patronage went almost exclusively to Esoteric Buddhist schools. Esoteric Buddhism was new to China at this point and relied on mysticism and ritual. Some historians have surmised that the mystical component may have appealed to the Taoist rulers, as Taoism also has elements of magical ritualism.

In direct contrast to the Lotus Sutra's doctrine that Buddhahood is present in all life and that all sentient beings can access it, the Esoteric schools hold that the Buddha's teachings for everyone are inferior to a set of secret, hidden teachings involving mantras (repeated mystical formulas), mudras (hand positions) and mandalas (objects of devotion) intended to fuse one's mind with the enlightenment of a Buddha called Mahavairochana.[10]

The Tiantai school was centered far from the imperial courts. Even had the Tang dynasty not favored the Esoteric schools, the Tiantai school was less likely to gain popularity with the ruling class because of the distance. In *The Flower of Chinese Buddhism*, SGI President Ikeda describes another reason the school had declined: "Foremost among the reasons for its eclipse was that the teachings of the Tiantai school were in a sense too profound and complex or too elevated in philosophical nature to be comprehensible to ordinary lay believers. This fact naturally made it difficult to propagate the Tiantai teachings on a wide scale and hindered the growth of the school" (p. 140).

Taking it upon himself to revitalize the popularity of the teachings and reassert the Lotus Sutra as supreme among all Buddhist teachings, Zhanran wrote several commentaries on Tiantai Zhiyi's writings. These commentaries fall into two categories, exegetical and polemical. The first category intended to clarify the meaning of Zhiyi's complicated works while the second used Zhiyi's teachings to refute those of the Flower Garland, Chan and Dharma Characteristics schools.

President Ikeda writes: "The polemical writings that resulted demonstrate, on the one hand, that Zhanran felt the need to refute what he saw as the error inherent in the teachings of these other schools and, on the other, his eagerness to convert others to the teachings of Tiantai. In a more profound sense, however, Zhanran's

polemic writing can be seen as the concern of a bodhisattva to propagate a teaching that promised salvation to all rather than only to the few" (*The Flower of Chinese Buddhism*, pp. 144–45).

Dengyo and the Formation of the Tendai School in Japan

Buddhism initially traveled from China to Japan via Korea, flourishing during the reign of Prince Shotoku,[11] the first Buddhist ruler of Japan. Shotoku enjoyed good diplomatic relations with the Sui dynasty (predecessors of the Tang) and encouraged exchange between Japanese and Chinese Buddhists. He established several Buddhist temples, of which Shittenno-ji in Osaka, built in 593, is the oldest.

In Tang dynasty China, the city of Chang'an was the center of Buddhist learning and imperial power. At that same time, Nara, then Japan's capital, held similar preeminence, and several Buddhist schools flourished there.

Saicho, known also by his posthumous title Dengyo, entered the Buddhist priesthood at 12. At a temple in Nara, he studied various forms of Buddhist philosophy, becoming particularly interested in the Tiantai school. In 788, he built a small thatched hut at Mount Hiei—adjacent to what in 794 would become Japan's new capital, Heian Kyo (today, Kyoto)—and devoted himself to further studies. He gained fame and support by lecturing to priests and nobles on Tiantai philosophy. He eventually earned the support of Emperor Kammu[12] and traveled to China, studying at Mount Tiantai. There he was taught by two of Miaole Zhanran's disciples, in addition to studying other forms of Buddhism with other teachers.

Upon his return, Dengyo set up Japan's first Tiantai school temple on Mount Hiei. This would later give rise to the Tendai[13] school, fully independent of the Chinese school. In addition to starting the Tendai school, Dengyo would frequently debate leaders of other Buddhist schools. He engaged in a lengthy, ongoing debate with Tokuitsu, a priest of the Dharma Characteristics school. Tokuitsu maintained

Dixon Hamby

Members of Super Leschi District in Seattle enjoy their monthly discussion meeting, June 2010.

that not everyone could attain Buddhahood. Dengyo asserted that all people possess a Buddha nature and that the Lotus Sutra was the Buddha's essential teaching.

According to Nichiren Daishonin, Dengyo's insistence on the Lotus Sutra's supremacy profoundly influenced the other Buddhist schools in Nara. He writes: "In the time of Emperor Kammu, the Great Teacher Dengyo refuted the Hinayana and provisional Mahayana teachings, and made clear the true significance of the Lotus Sutra. From that time on, opposing opinions ceased to prevail, and everyone single-mindedly put faith in the Lotus Sutra. Even those scholars of the earlier six schools [of Nara] who studied Hinayana and Mahayana teachings such as the Flower Garland, Wisdom, Profound Secrets, and Agama sutras regarded the Lotus Sutra as the ultimate authority" ("The Teaching, Capacity, Time, and Country," *The Writings of Nichiren Daishonin*, vol. 1, p. 52).

Dengyo's small hut on Mount Hiei became, in time, Enryaku-ji, the head Tendai temple and a major center of Buddhist learning at which many prominent Buddhists—several of whom went on to found their own schools—studied.

Esotericism in the Tendai Tradition

As with the Chinese Tiantai school, Tendai practice centered on doctrinal study of the Lotus Sutra and meditative practices designed to aid in perceiving one's inherent enlightenment. Dengyo had also studied Esoteric Buddhism during his time in China. Upon request of Emperor Kammu, some Esoteric Buddhist practices were incorporated. Thus, the Tendai school from its beginning differed from its Chinese counterpart. Despite this, Dengyo's focus was on the Lotus Sutra, but the influence of Esoteric doctrine within the Tendai school grew stronger with time. Dengyo's immediate successors also studied Esotericism in China, adding still more practices—such as the use of mudras, mantras, mandalas and rituals—into the Tendai doctrine.

Despite the Tendai school's popularity, differing opinions regarding its Esoteric components led to several schisms. Within a century and a half, thirteen Esoteric and two orthodox branches had formed.

Buddhism in the Kamakura Era

Tendai, along with the True Word school, which was based purely on esoteric tradition, dominated Japanese Buddhism for about three centuries. Other forms supplanted the Tendai school's popularity during the Kamakura era.[14] During this turbulent period, the True Word school remained powerful while the Tendai faltered.

The Pure Land teachings originated in China. In Japan, its teachings became popular within the Tendai school and a Pure Land school was formed under Honen, a former Tendai priest. The Pure Land school emphasized the worship of a Buddha named Amida,[15] who was said to reside in the "Pure Land of Perfect Bliss" located in the west. Practitioners pray, reciting a devotional phrase called the "Nembutsu,"[16] to be reborn in this land, and such rebirth, rather than enlightenment, is the goal of Pure Land practice.

Former Tendai priest Dogen popularized the Zen school, which had developed in China as the Chan school. Zen claims to come from a secret teaching transmitted wordlessly between Shakyamuni and his disciple Mahakashyapa. Practitioners of Zen seek emancipation through seated meditation, and Zen teachings were particularly popular among samurai and other members of the Kamakura shogunate.

The Precepts school, one of the first forms of Buddhism introduced to Japan, focused on the observation of monastic discipline harkening back to the earliest Buddhist schools in India. It declined in popularity while Tendai grew but regained some popularity in the Kamakura era. A division of the Precepts school became hybridized with Esoteric teachings during the Kamakura era, forming the True Word Precepts school.

Nichiren Daishonin's[17] Vow To Relieve the Suffering of All People

Zennichi-maro was born in 1222 in a small fishing village in Awa Province. In 1233, he entered nearby Seicho-ji, a small Tendai temple, in order to receive a general education. At that time, temples provided virtually the sole educational opportunity for children of the common classes, as there was no public school system. While studying at Seicho-ji, he prayed to a statue of Bodhisattva Space Treasury to become the wisest person in Japan.[18] His motive was to find a way to relieve the suffering wracking the people of his society. He said later that he gained a "jewel" of wisdom with which to clearly understand the essence of sutras.

He was ordained as a Tendai priest in 1237 and took the name Zesho-bo Rencho. He then traveled and studied at various temples, including at Mount Hiei. Applying his keen insight to the doctrinally convoluted world of Japanese Buddhism, he discerned which teachings were deep and which were shallow, which practices worked and which failed. As his inquiry progressed, he became increasingly convinced that the dominant forms of Japanese Buddhism were profoundly in error, and only the Lotus Sutra could lead people—all people—to enlightenment in the Latter Day of the Law.

On April 28, 1253, he lectured at Seicho-ji to an audience of priests and laity. On this occasion, he renamed himself Nichiren (Sun Lotus) and declared that the Lotus Sutra's essence could be found in chanting Nam-myoho-renge-kyo.[19] He also publicly criticized the Pure Land, or Nembutsu, school for denying the possibility of enlightenment in this life and this world and disparaging the Lotus Sutra, which advocated the enlightened potential of all people. Nichiren saw this school as a major cause of the people's miseries. Not only did he say that chanting the Nembutsu would not lead to the Pure Land (Nembutsu), he went so far as to say it led to the hell of incessant suffering, whereas chanting Nam-myoho-renge-kyo led to enlightenment in one's present lifetime.

This declaration incurred the wrath of local steward Tojo Kagenobu, a Nembutsu believer, who ordered Nichiren to be taken into custody. Nichiren escaped arrest on this occasion but over the years faced a series of harsh persecutions and accusations. He was ambushed, nearly beheaded and exiled twice, yet never ceased to broadly proclaim what he had realized, no matter the danger.

Paul Scharf

SGI-USA members travel to Boston University to attend the North Zone Youth Kick-off Meeting held at the university's Morse Auditorium, March 2010.

Refuting Error

Nichiren Daishonin writes: "In Buddhism, that teaching is judged supreme that enables all people, whether good or evil, to become Buddhas. Surely anyone can grasp so reasonable a standard. By means of this principle, we can compare the various sutras and ascertain which is superior. The Lotus Sutra reveals that even the people of the two vehicles can attain enlightenment, but the True Word sutras do not. Rather, they categorically deny it. The Lotus Sutra teaches that women are capable of attaining Buddhahood, but the True Word sutras make no mention of this at all. In the Lotus Sutra, it is written that evil people can attain enlightenment, but in the True Word sutras there is nothing about this. How can one say that the True Word sutras are superior to the Lotus Sutra?" ("Reply to Hoshina Goro Taro," WND-1, 156–57).

In this passage, Nichiren's standard for comparison is clear. Can a sutra lead all people to enlightenment or not? His principal criticisms of the four major schools of Kamakura-era Buddhism stem from this standard. First, aiming for rebirth in a pure land overlooks the problems people face in this world and rejects the possibility of attaining enlightenment in one's present form in this life. Zen claims to come from no sutra but rather a secret transmission. Why would Shakyamuni dedicate his life to the emancipation of all people only to teach the truth to one disciple in secret? The True Word schools also maintain secret rituals and doctrines. The Precepts school was grounded in adherence to disciplines that had lost any relevance and were beyond reason in their restrictiveness. As for Tendai, Nichiren said that despite the intention of its founders, the school had become nearly indistinguishable from Zen and Pure Land teachings.[20]

President Ikeda further elucidates what are called "the four dictums"—Nichiren's critique of these four schools of Buddhism:

> The four dictums are neither exclusivist nor intolerant. At their core is the Daishonin's reasoned religious criticism illuminated by the wisdom of the Mystic Law.
>
> In other words, on one level these four schools illustrate four unbalanced religious archetypes. The critique of them

therefore affords a glimpse of a fully developed religion as conceived by the Daishonin. This is a completely balanced teaching that harmoniously incorporates the fundamental characteristics of religion without bias or distortion. In a word, it is a religion for human beings.

The doctrines of these four schools can be summed up as: 1) salvation through the external power of an absolute being (Nembutsu); 2) attainment of enlightenment only through the direct perception of one's own mind and being content with that self-enlightenment (Zen); 3) gaining benefit in this life through occult means (True Word); 4) being controlled from without by means of precepts or standards (Precepts).

The perfectly balanced teaching does not succumb to any one of these extremes, but expounds the fusion of internal and external power as the means to transform the life of the individual, as well as the surrounding circumstances. Combining internal and external power means discovering within the self a power that is greater than the self. This is what is referred to in the Daishonin's teaching as "inherent" and "manifest" Buddhahood, and it is the essence of Nichiren Buddhism. (June 2002 *Living Buddhism*, pp. 16–17)

Revealing the True

Shakyamuni's realization of dependent origination, that all beings and phenomena arise based on their interconnected relationship with other beings and phenomena, was further explained by Nagarjuna as the three truths— non-substantiality, temporary existence and the Middle Way. Tiantai Zhiyi's analysis of Nagarjuna's work led to him perceiving the principle of "three thousand realms in a single moment of life" inherent in the Lotus Sutra. Zhiyi developed intense meditation methods designed to "observe the mind" and perceive the Buddha within.

Nichiren Daishonin writes, "The heart of the Lotus Sutra is the revelation that one may attain supreme enlightenment in one's present form without altering one's status as an ordinary person ("Reply to Hakiri Saburo," WND-1, 410). However effective Zhiyi's techniques, the capacity and years of intensive practice required push them well beyond the reach of most people.

Nichiren identified chanting Nam-myoho-renge-kyo as the practice for perceiving the fundamental nature of life. He saw that it encompasses and clarifies the teachings of Shakyamuni, Nagarjuna and Tiantai Zhiyi, and, most important, it is a practice accessible to all.

Though Kamakura-era Buddhist schools placed greater importance on the laity than had earlier Japanese schools, they still centered primarily on the role of the clergy and the patronage of the nobility. Nichiren's followers came from every level of Japanese society, from the poorest classes to farmers, samurai, wealthy lords and priests. His high regard for women and his insistence that the Lotus Sutra guarantees their enlightenment is particularly notable and was virtually unheard of in his day.

Shortly after surviving the execution attempt on the beach at Tatsunokuchi, Nichiren took to inscribing mandalas for his followers. Nichiren's mandala—the Gohonzon—is a graphic expression of enlightenment itself. It reads "Nam-myoho-renge-kyo Nichiren" down the center and is flanked on either side by characters representing the "mutual possession of the Ten Worlds"[21] and the Ceremony in the Air.[22]

The practice of chanting Nam-myoho-renge-kyo to the Gohonzon has similarities and differences with practices of other Buddhist schools. Unlike the mandalas of the Esoteric schools, which venerated the nonhuman Buddha Mahavairochana, the Gohonzon venerates the Law of life itself, the Buddha nature within all beings. Nichiren referred to it as "the object of devotion for observing the mind," meaning that in devotion to it, one perceives and brings forth his or her own enlightened life-condition. The Pure Land school also advocated chanting a phrase, but in their case it is to the external, imaginary Buddha, Amida. The school relies exclusively on salvation through an outside power. Chanting

Nam-myoho-renge-kyo is directed outward and inward; through awakening the Buddha nature within, one perceives the connection of all life. Chanting is a means of self-reflection as well, in that it has a meditative component. But unlike Zen meditation, which focuses on mental insight, the meditative aspect of chanting Nam-myoho-renge-kyo focuses on activating the dynamic qualities of Buddhahood at the core of our physical, spiritual and mental being. As for precepts, Nichiren said their purpose is to prevent error and to put an end to evil. Thus, for his followers, upholding faith in the Lotus Sutra by chanting Nam-myoho-renge-kyo to the Gohonzon is the sole precept that must be observed, as doing so gives one the insight, life force, courage and wisdom to recognize and defeat evil (see *The Record of the Orally Transmitted Teachings*, pp. 99–100).

Another crucial difference between Nichiren's teachings and those of the other schools of his day is the principle of "establishing the correct teaching for the peace of the land."[23] Peace and security on a national or even global level, according to Nichiren, derives from a profound transformation in the life of each person that results from embracing the essential teaching and discarding erroneous teachings. Buddhist practice, he taught, was for oneself and others, and creating a peaceful world through the widespread propagation of the Lotus Sutra is a cornerstone of his teachings, one that he repeatedly risked his life to proclaim.

—*Prepared by* Living Buddhism

1. See pp. 26–27 for more on Nagarjuna.

2. *The Flower of Chinese Buddhism* uses the Pinyin method of Chinese transliteration. Tiantai Zhiyi is the Pinyin spelling whereas T'ien-t'ai Chih-i is of the older Wade-Giles method. See pp. 32–34 for more on Tiantai Zhiyi.

3. Tang dynasty: A dynasty in China that lasted from 618 to 907 BCE.

4. Laozi: also known as Lao-tzu. Taoist philosopher, considered the author of the *Daodejing* (Classic of the Way), a central Taoist scripture.

5. Miaole Zhanran (711–82): Also spelled Miao-lo Chan-jan in Wade-Giles.

6. The sixth patriarch of the Tiantai school: This classification derives from the tradition that counts Tiantai Zhiyi as the first patriarch of the school. It is also possible to consider him the ninth patriarch in the tradition that counts Nagarjuna as the founder.

7. Chan: Also known as "Dhyana" in Sanskrit or "Zen" in Japanese. A Buddhist school advocating attainment of enlightenment through meditation rather than doctrinal study.

8. Dharma Characteristics: A branch of the Consciousness-Only school that sought to clarify the true nature of reality by analyzing and classifying phenomena.

9. Flower Garland: A Chinese Buddhist school based on the Flower Garland Sutra.

10. Mahavairochana: A Buddha said to personify the unchanging truth of phenomena. Mahavairochana is not an actual historical Buddha.

11. Prince Shotoku (574–662): Also known as Prince Umayado. A member of the ruling Soga clan, he was appointed regent in 593 by Empress Suiko, who decided to abstain from politics and delegated all powers to him. He is known for being instrumental in bringing aspects of Chinese culture and society into Japan, such as the form of writing, form of government and beliefs in Buddhism. He composed commentaries on the Lotus Sutra and two other sutras.

12. Emperor Kammu (737–806): Reigned 781–806. Though he opposed the Buddhist establishment's economic and political power, he became a generous patron of monks Saicho (Dengyo) and Kukai (Kobo Daishi). He was a vigorous ruler, and the throne's power and prestige peaked during his reign.

13. Tendai is the Japanese pronunciation of Tiantai.

14. Kamakura era (1185–1333): A time in which military rule all but replaced imperial rule. In 1180, the warrior government organization headed by Minamoto no Yoritomo was established in Kamakura, and in 1185, the power structure for maintaining control over the country was set up. The main seat of power resided in Kamakura while the imperial court remained in Kyoto.

15. Amida: The Buddha of the Pure Land of Perfect Bliss in the west. Like Mahavairochana, Amida is not an actual historical Buddha.

16. Nembutsu: Literally meaning "meditation on a Buddha, interpreted to mean reciting the name of a Buddha," especially that of Amida Buddha. The practice of the Pure Land school is to recite the invocation Namu Amida Butsu ("Homage to Amida Buddha").

17. A full and detailed biography of Nichiren Daishonin is beyond the scope of this article. Please see pp. 54–65.

18. See "Letter to the Priests of Seicho-ji," WND-1, 650–53.

19. Nam-myoho-renge-kyo containing the entire meaning of the Lotus Sutra is exhaustively documented in *The Record of the Orally Transmitted Teachings*.

20. See "The Tripitaka Master Shan-wu-wei," WND-1, 176.

21. Mutual possession of the Ten Worlds: The principle that each of the Ten Worlds from hell to Buddhahood possesses the potential for the nine others within itself.

22. Ceremony in the Air: A scene in the Lotus Sutra described over the course of 11 chapters of the sutra, beginning with "Emergence of the Treasure Tower," in which the assembly is suspended midair. See also "The Real Aspect of the Gohonzon," WND-1, 831–34.

23. See "On Establishing the Correct Teaching for the Peace of the Land," WND-1, 6–32.

History *of* Buddhist
HUMANISM

*Key Buddhist philosophers and
reformers leading up to the founding
presidents of the SGI*

NICHIREN BUDDHISM and the CREATION of the SOKA GAKKAI

Nichiren Daishonin died in 1282 while visiting his disciple Ikegami Munenaka in Musashi Province (present-day Tokyo). He'd become increasingly ill after many years of hardship. About a month before his death, he set his affairs in order, designating his longtime disciple Nikko as his successor and five others as senior priests. He specified that Nikko should be the "great guide and teacher in the spread of the essential teaching" ("The Minobu Transfer Document," *The Writings of Nichiren Daishonin*, vol. 2, p. 993). In another document, written a few weeks later, Nikko was also designated the superintendent of Kuon-ji on Mount Minobu, a temple Nichiren had built with his disciples (see "The Ikegami Transfer Document," WND-2, 996).

Nikko faced difficulties soon after Nichiren's death. Hakiri Sanenaga, steward of Minobu, whom Nikko had personally introduced to Nichiren's teachings, worshipped a statue of Shakyamuni Buddha in addition to making pilgrimages and giving monetary support to temples of the Pure Land and True Word schools. This was a direct contradiction of Nichiren's teaching, as the Gohonzon is the only object of devotion for Nichiren's disciples. Nikko tried to correct Sanenaga, but the steward would not change his ways.

Sanenaga had, in fact, come under the influence of Niko,[1] one of the other senior priests. Niko, it seems, had deviated from Nichiren's teachings regarding the error and slander of the established religious schools, and had ignored Nichiren's admonitions not to present those schools with offerings. Niko permitted priests and laity to visit and make offerings to Shinto shrines and other schools' temples. He commissioned an esoteric mandala to be painted at the home of a lay believer and then conducted a sermon about the mandala, getting drunk afterword and singing vulgar songs.

The senior priests' other slanders include selling Gohonzon inscribed by Nichiren or hanging them behind statues of Shakyamuni. The priests said that Nichiren's teachings belonged to the Tendai school, though Nichiren had clearly left that school early on. They also destroyed some of Nichiren's letters. Eminent Buddhists of the time were expected to write only in classical Chinese, but Nichiren, writing to lay believers of all social classes, often wrote in ordinary Japanese using the phonetic script accessible to the general public. Some senior priests evidently found Nichiren's use of common writing forms embarrassing.

Nikko left Minobu in 1289, distancing himself from the slanders of Niko and Sanenaga, and clearly departing from the other senior priests who had committed acts counter to Nichiren's teachings and had shirked duties such as the maintenance of Nichiren's gravesite. Nikko, after trying and failing to straighten out the priests, moved with his supporters to land donated by Nanjo Tokimitsu, a longtime supporter of Nichiren, at the base of Mount Fuji. There, he established the Omosu Seminary and focused primarily on propagation, instruction and writing.

Buddhism in Feudal Japan

A month before his death in 1333, when he was 88, Nikko set down a list of critical guidelines called *The Twenty-six Admonitions*,[2] intended to address deviations from Nichiren Daishonin's teachings that Nikko observed in his disciples or saw as potential pitfalls for future disciples. He wished to set clear warnings for future generations as well, writing, "I have set forth these 26 articles for the sake of the eternal salvation and protection of humankind" (*Gosho zenshu*, p. 1619).

The first admonition states, "The doctrines of the Fuji school must not differ in the least from the teachings of the late master." Other admonitions include warnings against forged documents purported to be written by Nichiren, warnings against priests and laity visiting shrines of other schools, and encouragement to study Nichiren's writings and avoid shallow pursuits of fame or idle pastimes.

Despite Nikko's strict adherence to the example set by Nichiren, the Fuji school faltered not long after Nikko's passing.[3] They frequently forgot or ignored the spirit of their founder, Nichiren, to spread the Law courageously among all people.

The Buddhist practice for laity, especially for the common classes, became less about individual emancipation from suffering and increasingly about supporting priests. As we have seen in previous installments of this series, this is hardly a unique occurrence in Buddhist history. Rather, it is part of a well-established pattern.

Nichiren's teachings are clearly intended for all people to practice and thereby transform their lives. Nevertheless, the schools that claimed to teach and preserve Nichiren Buddhism have a shoddy record at best when it comes to supporting the laity in their practice. Nichiren writes that his aim is to "awaken all the people of Japan to faith in the Lotus Sutra so that they too can share the heritage and attain Buddhahood" ("The Heritage of the Ultimate Law of Life," WND-1, 217). Despite this and other direct statements of his desire to spread the Law to all people, the Fuji school in later years created the doctrine that the heritage of the Law had been passed only from Nichiren to Nikko and from Nikko to his successor Nichimoku, and so on, forming an unbroken link of mystical transmission of the Law from high priest to high priest. They claim, to this day, that only the high priest can truly inherit the Law and becomes infallible upon doing so. Despite having no doctrinal basis for this belief, they continue to support an idea of exclusive powers granted upon transmission and a supernatural connection to Nichiren.

The appeal of Kamakura Buddhist schools among commoners diminished as the focus shifted from propagation to involvement in secular affairs. During centuries of ongoing civil war and feudalism after the Kamakura era, Buddhist schools became increasingly enmeshed in the workings of the shogunate. The Tendai school, centered at Mount Hiei, became militaristic. Though Buddhism is naturally opposed to violence, the Tendai school at times armed its monks, who battled with other schools, as well as with soldiers.[4] Zen, which had always enjoyed popularity among the samurai, rapidly became the most influential school. Zen priests often acted as civic and military advisors to government officials, and as a result, Zen schools were well funded. The Nichiren schools at Fuji and Minobu were involved in local politics, though they were not significant on a national level.

Ratchana Jaey Akarapolpaisansin

Members in Atlanta enjoy a meeting commemorating
SGI-USA Men's Division Day on August 24, 2010.

In the 17th century, all Buddhist schools fell under what is called the parish system. Following a Japanese Christian revolt in 1638, the government required all Japanese citizens to register with a local Buddhist temple to prove they were not Christian. Without registering, citizens were not allowed to work or travel. This gave the priests who ran the temples significant authority over local politics and guaranteed them a stable group of lay supporters. The government also banned public religious debate. Thus, it became very difficult for an ordinary citizen to leave one temple and join another, or to even hear of the teachings of another school. The propagation of Buddhist teachings ground to a halt even as the temples grew in power.

Under the parish system, Buddhist funerals were required for parishioners' family members. Donations for funeral services, interment, the granting of posthumous Buddhist names and the inscription of wooden memorial *toba* tablets to be displayed at the gravesite became a substantial source of income for temples. As a result, Buddhism under the parish system later came to be referred to by the epithet *funeral Buddhism*. Even today, the vast majority of Japanese people, regardless of religious affiliation in life, have Buddhist funerals. Also, the Japanese word

jobutsu, meaning "to attain enlightenment," has come to be a synonym for "to die."

Taiseki-ji was declared the head temple of the Fuji school (later known as Nichiren Shoshu). Under parish system law, the Fuji school ceased propagation and focused instead on registration and rituals, praying on behalf of lay believers who made donations, rather than encouraging the laity to practice for themselves.

Nichikan

In 1683, the 15-year-old son of a Tokugawa retainer entered the priesthood at Taiseki-ji. Ito Ichinoshin, later known as Nichikan, excelled at Buddhist study and was appointed as a lecturer at Hosokusa Seminary.[5] In 1718, he became chief priest of Taiseki-ji.

Nichikan lamented the state of the Fuji school, which he considered rife with error, and sought to correct the many misinterpretations of Nichiren's teachings that abounded in the school. He denied the idea that a high priest is infallible and said that meritorious deeds, rather than transmission, determine a priest's worth. The behavior of the school's priests at this point little resembled that of Nichiren's immediate successor, Nikko.

The 15th through 23rd high priests of the Fuji school had come from Yobo-ji, a temple that mixed Fuji school doctrines and its own interpretations. For example, 17th high priest Nissei taught that statues of Shakyamuni were equal to the Gohonzon.

The Untold History of the Fuji School summarizes Nichikan's activities as follows:

> By the time Nichikan became high priest, some four hundred years after the Daishonin's passing, Nichiren schools had distorted his teachings and promulgated various misinterpretations. Through the *Six-volume Writings*, Nichikan reestablished the orthodoxy of Nichiren Buddhism as transmitted to his legitimate successor, Nikko Shonin.
>
> According to "The Accounts of High Priest Nichikan," when Nichikan bestowed the *Six-volume Writings* on his disciples, he stated: "With these six volumes of writing, which are like the lion king, you need not be afraid of the various sects and schools in the nation even if they all come to this temple for debate like a pack of foxes . . ."[6]
>
> Nichikan believed that the purpose of Buddhist study was to propagate Nichiren Buddhism. In the beginning of "The Threefold Secret Teaching," he states: "There are many important matters in this writing. This I did solely to perpetuate the Law. My disciples should deeply understand my intention.[7] (pp. 70–71)

Central to Nichikan's reform was his emphasis on the Gohonzon as the object of devotion through which all people can attain enlightenment. He writes: "Everyone who receives and embraces this object of devotion enters the way of the Buddha of time without beginning . . . And we common mortals who have entered the way of this Buddha are entirely one with this Buddha of limitless joy. The Buddha of limitless joy is entirely one with us common mortals. How could this not indicate the oneness of mentor and disciple?" (see *My Dear Friends in America*, second edition, p. 303).

Buddhism During the Meiji Restoration

The 19th century saw the end of the shogunate and samurai rule and the return of imperial power during the Meiji Restoration. With this came tumultuous social changes and a resurgence of nationalism leading to military campaigns against China, Korea and Russia. The Meiji government, though nationalistic, was not isolationist. Japan vigorously reopened trade with the West. Western food, dress, art, literature and customs became popular.

Shinto was made the state religion, while the government subordinated the role of Buddhism in its affairs; and many schools faced outright persecution. Out of an imperial desire to control and alter Buddhism, in 1872, the government declared that Buddhist priests were permitted to marry, eat meat, grow their hair and dress in secular clothing.

Rather than resist the changes made by secular authority, the major Japanese Buddhist schools not only capitulated but also vocally supported the new nationalistic and militaristic government. Nichiren Buddhist schools were no exception.

The Beginnings of the Soka Gakkai

Educator and author Tsunesaburo Makiguchi was born in 1871. Like other intellectuals of his time, he expressed a fondness for Western thinkers, especially educational reformer John Dewey, and saw the industrialization of Japan as a potentially positive move. He cannot, however, be considered a nationalist, as he held decidedly global views, emphasizing the interconnectedness of life.

In the first chapter of his book *A Geography of Human Life*, he states, "I am astonished at the

Rob Hendry

Members of Arnold District in Maryland commemorate SGI-USA's women's month, February 2010.

broad origins of the objects that affect my life" (p. 11). He then relates that the wool he wears is from South America or Australia and processed in England while his shoes are made mostly of Indian leather except for the American leather sole. He writes, "It would be foolish to narrow our vision to our own small portion of the world. (p. 13).

In 1928, Mr. Makiguchi became a lay follower of Nichiren Shoshu (as the Fuji school had renamed itself in the late 19th century). He founded the Soka Kyoiku Gakkai (Value-Creating Education Society, predecessor to the Soka Gakkai) with Josei Toda and several other educators in 1930.[8] Though the group began with a primarily pedagogical agenda, it became increasingly concerned with Nichiren Buddhism as a philosophy that could revitalize ordinary people's lives.

The wartime Japanese government required all religious groups to enshrine a Shinto talisman, a symbol of the Sun Goddess that was central to Shinto worship. Mr. Makiguchi and Mr. Toda refused to accept the talisman, and they did so in contrast to the Nichiren Shoshu priests, who buckled under government pressure. As a result, Mr. Makiguchi and Mr. Toda were jailed. Mr. Makiguchi died behind bars at age 73 after two years of imprisonment and harsh interrogation.

Just before the official end of World War II, Mr. Toda was released. Religious freedom was established in Japan under the American occupation. Many new religious groups emerged in the postwar chaos, as the Japanese people sought relief from their suffering not only from the loss of the war and a crushed national identity but also from rampant poverty and food shortages.

During his incarceration, Mr. Toda had gained profound insight into the Lotus Sutra. Though the Nichiren Shoshu priests, before and after the war, had done little to spread Nichiren's teachings, Mr. Toda made a profound vow to widely propagate them.

Nichiren Buddhism grew rapidly because of President Toda's leadership and the Soka Gakkai members' enthusiasm. For the first time in history, a broad movement of lay practitioners was propagating the Lotus Sutra. Its membership was energetic and hopeful, a bright contrast to the centuries of Japanese Buddhism's morbid formality. The members took personal responsibility for their own Buddhist practice rather than relying on priests to pray for them.

Since Soka Gakkai members were then affiliated with Nichiren Shoshu, the school grew to an unprecedented level. The Soka Gakkai provided substantial donations, renovated the head temple and built hundreds of local temples.

Some in the priesthood genuinely appreciated both the financial support and the fresh vigor that came with the Soka Gakkai's expansion, but others were less pleased. Soka Gakkai members on their own fulfilled many functions that had once been the sole domain of the clergy. The lay believers propagated the teachings, recited the sutra and chanted Nam-myoho-renge-kyo every day. Mr. Toda collaborated with retired high priest Nichiko Hori to compile and publish Nichiren's writings as the *Gosho zenshu*, giving the laity and the general public a basis for studying Nichiren's writings. Soka Gakkai members studied and lectured on Buddhist topics. Nichiren Shoshu had barely grown in its 700 years; the Soka Gakkai made it an international religious movement.

The relationship between the Soka Gakkai and the leadership of the Nichiren Shoshu priesthood, while never entirely without tension, changed significantly when Nikken Abe became the high priest in 1979. The membership of the international organization remained generally unaware of the growing difficulties. Nikken, in fact, publicly praised the SGI and its leaders, while privately he schemed to dismantle the organization's leadership. Daisaku Ikeda, the third Soka Gakkai president, tried repeatedly to address the difficulties through dialogue but was often denied the opportunity, especially toward the end of the 1980s.

The Soka Gakkai leaders were long aware of the machinations of Nichiren Shoshu priests, who were motivated by greed and desire for power. In the 1950s, long before Nikken came to power, President Toda wrote an essay comparing priests to geisha, saying that while both performed services for money, at least geisha were cheerful. Nevertheless, the Soka Gakkai supported the priesthood out of respect for the school's founders, Nichiren Daishonin and Nikko Shonin.

President Ikeda writes: "We protected the priesthood with utmost sincerity. In recent years, as well, even while confronted with the reality of the decadence and runaway greed of priests, we have all along made known our wish that the priesthood purify itself" (June 8, 1992, *World Tribune*, p. 5).

Nikken had maneuvered for years to denigrate President Ikeda, especially with the help of a former Soka Gakkai attorney, Masatomo Yamazaki. Yamazaki helped stage multiple media attacks against President Ikeda and colluded with anti-Soka Gakkai factions in the Japanese government who feared its populist movement.

In November 1991, Nikken ordered the Soka Gakkai to disband, excommunicating the leadership, and later, the entire membership. He claimed that the high priest is directly connected to Nichiren and that the laity cannot hope for emancipation from suffering without the high priest's blessing. He also claimed that the Gohonzon would not function without a ceremony performed by a high priest. Of course, Nichiren taught nothing like this, and the vast majority of the SGI membership—as well as a number of priests within Nichiren Shoshu—recognized Nikken's views as a serious perversion of doctrine.

Nichiren never taught that the heritage of the Law is a mystical property handed down from priest to priest. Rather it is found in faith and the shared struggle to spread the Buddha's teachings. He writes:

> All disciples and lay supporters of Nichiren should chant Nam-myoho-renge-kyo with the spirit of many in body but one in mind, transcending all differences among themselves to become as inseparable as fish and the water in which they swim. This spiritual bond is the basis for the universal transmission of the ultimate Law of life and death. Herein lies the true goal of Nichiren's propagation. ("The Heritage of the Ultimate Law of Life," WND-1, 217)

The attempt to destroy the Soka Gakkai through priestly authority can only be called a failure. The Soka Gakkai did not disband. Rather, liberated from decades of funding and supporting the priesthood, it flourished. The Soka Gakkai had always emphasized Nichiren's teaching that practitioners take responsibility in faith, practice and study. As a result, the self-sufficient laity had no real need for priests.

The SGI and Buddhist Humanism

President Ikeda encapsulates the heart of Buddhist humanism as follows:

> Shakyamuni, who believed in continually seeking self-improvement, plunged into the realities of society as an "educator" in pursuit of a truly human way of life, not as an absolute being who looked down on the people.
>
> The founder and first president of the Soka Gakkai, Tsunesaburo Makiguchi, fought against Japanese militarism and died in prison as a result at age seventy-three. "We must never submit to inhumane authority," he cried. "Toward that end, we, each one of us, must awaken to the supremely precious brilliance that lies within the depths of human life. And we must enlarge the circle of solidarity for peace." With his heart thus ablaze, he persevered to the end in the struggle to bring about a human revolution in the depths of people's lives, with dialogue as his weapon.
>
> It is my conviction that major progress in the development of a humane society may be realized by generating increasing trust in, and understanding for, humanism. (*My Dear Friends in America*, second edition, p. 334)

In the Lotus Sutra, Shakyamuni Buddha states: "At all times I think to myself: / How can I cause living beings / to gain entry into the unsurpassed way / and quickly acquire the body of a buddha?" (*The Lotus Sutra and Its Opening and Closing Sutras*, p. 273). Throughout this series, we have seen that the Buddhist order has, over the centuries, both distorted and restored the Buddha's fundamental vow of Buddhahood for all. Distortions arise because of the three poisons—greed, anger and foolishness. Restoration and reform require courage, compassion and wisdom.

Following Nichiren Daishonin's teachings, the SGI has created an unprecedented place in history. Never before has such a diverse, unified and egalitarian lay organization of Buddhists spread the Lotus Sutra's ideals throughout the world. Before the 1960s, Buddhism was not well known outside of Asia, and Nichiren's teachings were scarcely known at all. Buddhism's emergence as a world religion is due, on one hand, to various sociopolitical factors. On the other hand, it has spread because of the efforts of ordinary people. With President Ikeda paving the way, SGI members in particular have had a major impact on the spread of Buddhism, bringing the humanistic philosophy of Nichiren Daishonin to 192 countries and territories.

—Prepared by Living Buddhism

---

1. Though Nikko and Niko sound very similar to English speakers, the Chinese characters that make up their names are distinct.

2. See sokaspirit.org for the full list of *The Twenty-six Admonitions*, as well as SGI President Ikeda's analysis of them.

3. For a detailed account of the errors the Fuji school committed, please see *The Untold History of the Fuji School*.

4. The Tendai school was all but destroyed in the 15th century when warlord Oda Nobunaga, partly in an effort to curry favor with Christian nations in the West, led an attack on Mount Hiei.

5. Hosokusa Seminary: a school established jointly by the Fuji school and another Nichiren Buddhist school called Eight Chapters. Eight Chapters, Fuji and several other Nichiren schools formally merged in 1874 and then split again two years later.

6. *Fuji-shugaku-yoshu* (Essential Writings of the Fuji School), vol. 5, pp. 355–56.

7. *Rokkan-sho* (Six-volume Writings), p. 3.

8. The history of the Soka Gakkai is thoroughly chronicled elsewhere, and this article focuses on specific aspects rather than restating the history in detail. For further reading, please see pp. 66–85 in this book, as well as *The Human Revolution* and *The New Human Revolution* series.

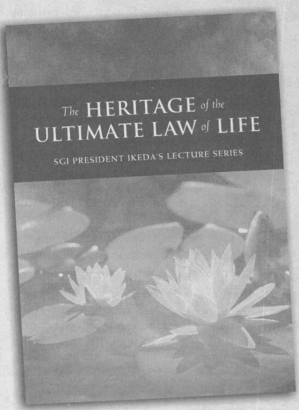

THE NEW HUMAN REVOLUTION

DAISAKU IKEDA
VOLUME 22

THE NEW HUMAN REVOLUTION

VOLUME 22

On July 23, 1975, SGI President Ikeda attended the opening ceremony of the control center that was set up for the Blue Hawaii Convention. After cutting the ribbon, he spoke to those present about the workplace.

"It's very important to give it your full effort, become the top performer in your workplace and win the trust of those around you . . .

"Each morning, you should pray with determination to do your best at your job that day, become a victor in your workplace and demonstrate the power of your Buddhist faith. That's the key to fully manifesting your greatest strength and wisdom. When you find a new job, please adopt that attitude, do your best and become a victor in the workplace. That's the Soka Gakkai spirit" (pp. 103–04).

SKU # 275453 • $12.00

Available at all SGI-USA bookstores or purchase copies via mail order:
(800) 626-1313

or shop online by visiting **sgi-usa.org** and clicking on "SGI-USA Online Store"

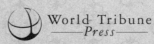
World Tribune *Press*

OTHER VOLUMES:

vol. 1	4601	$12.00	vol. 14	4614	$12.00
vol. 2	4602	$12.00	vol. 15	275446	$12.00
vol. 3	4603	$12.00	vol. 16	275447	$12.00
vol. 4	4604	$10.00	vol. 17	275448	$12.00
vol. 5	4605	$10.00	vol. 18	275449	$12.00
vol. 6	4606	$12.00	vol. 19	275450	$12.00
vol. 7	4607	$12.00	vol. 20	275451	$12.00
vol. 8	4608	$12.00	vol. 21	275452	$12.00
vol. 9	4609	$12.00			
vol. 10	4610	$12.00			
vol. 11	4611	$12.00			
vol. 12	4612	$12.00			
vol. 13	4613	$12.00			

THE LIFE OF
NICHIREN DAISHONIN

This is the first of a two-part article on the life of Nichiren Daishonin. This first installment takes readers from Nichiren's early years to his transformational experience during the Tatsunokuchi Persecution.

NICHIREN DAISHONIN devoted his life to a compassionate struggle to spread the Mystic Law based on a vow to enable all people to open within themselves the life-state of a Buddha.

At the same time, his was a life spent challenging and calling to account those forces that

sought to obstruct the happiness of ordinary people. In the process, he met and overcame a continuous series of major obstacles and persecutions.

HIS EARLY YEARS

Nichiren Daishonin, whose childhood name was Zennichi-maro, was born on February 16,

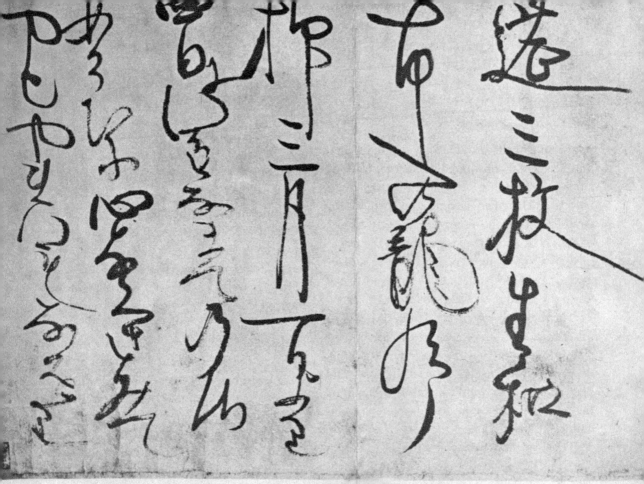

A sample of Nichiren Daishonin's handwritten letter "On the Three Seating Mats" (WND-2, 991).

1222, in Awa Province (in modern-day Chiba Prefecture, Japan). His father made a living as a fisherman, and therefore his family belonged to the class of common laborers.

At 12, Zennichi-maro entered Seicho-ji temple, a Buddhist temple in Awa, to obtain the equivalent of an elementary school education. During this period, he prayed "to become the wisest person in Japan" ("Letter to the Priests of Seicho-ji," *The Writings of Nichiren Daishonin*, vol. 1, p. 650).

He resolved to fully grasp and embody in his own life the deepest wisdom of Buddhism, so that he might lead his parents and all people to overcome the fundamental sufferings associated with living and dying. To accomplish this, he decided to become a Buddhist monk and to thoroughly pursue the Buddhist teachings.

In 1237, he was formally ordained as a Buddhist priest and took the name Zesho-bo Rencho. Studying under Dozen-bo, a priest at Seicho-ji, he described having been bestowed during that time "a jewel of wisdom as bright as the morning star" ("The Tripitaka Master Shan-wu-wei," WND-1, 176). By this, he was referring to the wisdom that would enable him to discover and fully grasp the wonderful teaching, or Mystic Law, that could rightly be called the essence or foundation of all Buddhist teachings.

Nichiren then embarked on a quest to visit and study at the various major Buddhist temples of Kamakura, Kyoto and Nara. In the process, he carefully read through all the Buddhist sutras these temples housed and researched the essential doctrines of the major Buddhist schools.

THE ESTABLISHMENT OF HIS TEACHINGS

As a result of these studies, he concluded that the Lotus Sutra constituted the highest teaching among the Buddhist sutras and that the Mystic Law to which he had become awakened was the Law of Nam-myoho-renge-kyo, the very essence of the Lotus Sutra. Regarding this as the teaching capable of saving all people of the Latter Day of the Law[1] from suffering, he resolved that it was his mission to spread it widely.

Through his intensive studies, he confirmed his mission as well as the method by which he would propagate that teaching. Prepared to meet the great difficulties and persecutions that would certainly arise along the way, he determined to commence propagating the Mystic Law.

Then, around noon on April 28, 1253, at Seicho-ji, he spoke publicly, refuting the teachings of the Pure Land and other major Buddhist schools of Japan. He chanted Nam-myoho-renge-kyo in a strong voice, and declared it to be the one and only correct teaching capable of saving all people of the Latter Day of the Law. This event is known as Nichiren's declaration of the establishment of his teaching. On that occasion, at age 32, he set forth for the first time the essential elements of his teachings and gave himself the name *Nichiren*, composed of the Chinese characters for *sun* and *lotus*.

In declaring his teaching, Nichiren strictly criticized the self-righteous doctrine of the Pure Land, or Nembutsu, school [which taught that chanting the name of Amida Buddha—a Buddha said to inhabit a pure land in the western reaches of the cosmos—would gain one salvation in the next life, in Amida's pure land. *Nembutsu* means to "contemplate the Buddha" and refers to the chanting of the phrase "Namu Amida Butsu"].

Tojo Kagenobu, the steward of the area where Seicho-ji was located, was a strong Pure Land believer, and he became enraged upon hearing about Nichiren's criticism of the Pure Land teachings. Intent on harming the Daishonin, he sent his men to Seicho-ji to capture him. But with the help of Dozen-bo and other priests at the temple, Nichiren escaped unharmed. He then went to Kamakura, where he took up residence in a simple lodging in Matsubagayatsu of the Nagoe district and commenced activities to propagate his teaching.

While spreading the practice of chanting Nam-myoho-renge-kyo, Nichiren continued to refute the errors of the Pure Land and Zen schools. In his view, these schools, which had become widely popular, exerted a negative influence on the people of Kamakura.

As a result of his propagation efforts, such figures as Toki Jonin, Shijo Kingo and Ikegami Munenaka—who remained his devoted followers throughout life—took faith in the Daishonin's teachings.

REMONSTRATION WITH THE GOVERNMENT INCURS PERSECUTIONS

Natural disasters and climatic disturbances such as extreme weather and earthquakes, as well as famine, fires and epidemics, had successively struck Japan at the rate of nearly one such calamity every year.

In particular, a major earthquake struck Kamakura in August 1257, causing widespread destruction.

This disaster and its aftermath served as an impetus for Nichiren to resolve to illuminate, through Buddhism, the fundamental causes for the miseries besetting his society and to clarify the means to eradicate those causes. To that end, he went to Jisso-ji temple in Iwamoto (in present-day Shizuoka Prefecture) and made an intensive study of all the Buddhist sutras and texts in the temple's sutra library. It was during his studies at Jisso-ji that he encountered the young man who would in due course be called Nikko and become his closest disciple and direct successor.

Using what he had gleaned from his research, Nichiren authored a treatise titled "On Establishing the Correct Teaching for the Peace of the Land" (Jpn *Rissho ankoku ron*; see WND-1, 6). On July, 16, 1260, he submitted this work to Hojo Tokiyori, the retired regent and de-facto ruler at the time.

This was Nichiren's first official remonstration with the sovereign.

In "On Establishing the Correct Teaching," Nichiren identifies the cause of the continuing onslaught of natural disasters and other calamities assailing the nation. He attributes it to the fact that people throughout the land had for some time been placing their belief in erroneous and misleading Buddhist teachings; the most culpable among these teachings, he points out, is the Pure Land school.

Should the people cease their donations to and support of such evil doctrines and embrace the correct teaching of the Lotus Sutra, he emphasizes, they can establish a land of peace and security.

If, however, they continue to lend support to misleading teachings, then, of the three calamities and seven disasters[2] that various sutras say will beset a land hostile to the correct Buddhist teaching, the two catastrophes that have yet to occur—"revolt within one's own domain" and "invasion from foreign lands"—will ultimately appear.

The Daishonin admonishes the people to quickly take faith in the correct teaching of the

Lotus Sutra and cease their support of erroneous teachings.

The leaders of the Kamakura shogunate ignored Nichiren's earnest remonstration. Additionally, priests of the Pure Land school, with the tacit support of powerful individuals in the government, conspired to have Nichiren persecuted.

On the evening of August 27, 1260, a group of Pure Land believers, intent on killing Nichiren, attacked his dwelling at Matsubagayatsu. Fortunately, the Daishonin was not present during the attack, and he subsequently decided to leave Kamakura for a time.

On May 12, 1261, after his return to Kamakura, the shogunate arrested Nichiren and exiled him to Ito on the Izu Peninsula. This came to be known as the Izu Exile.

In February 1263, he was pardoned from exile in Izu and returned again to Kamakura. The next year, he set out for his home province of Awa to visit his ailing mother.

On November 11, 1264, while on the way to the estate of his follower Kudo Yoshitaka in Amatsu of Awa Province, Nichiren and his party were attacked by a group of warriors led by the local steward, Tojo Kagenobu (the same steward who had sought to attack him when he first declared his teaching at Seicho-ji in 1253). Nichiren's disciple Kyonin-bo was killed in the attack, and Kudo Yoshitaka died later of his wounds; Nichiren himself received a deep cut on his forehead and had his left hand broken. This attack is known as the Komatsubara Persecution.

THE TATSUNOKUCHI PERSECUTION: "CASTING OFF THE TRANSIENT TO REVEAL THE TRUE"

In 1268, an official letter from the ruler of the Mongol empire arrived in Kamakura. It conveyed the Mongols' intention to use military force against Japan should Japanese leaders not respond to their demands for submission and payment of tribute. With this, the prediction of the calamity of invasion from foreign lands that Nichiren Daishonin had predicted in "On Establishing the Correct Teaching for the Peace of the Land" would soon be fulfilled.

After learning of this news, Nichiren sent letters of remonstration to 11 key figures in Kamakura, including the regent, Hojo Tokimune, and priests representing major Buddhist temples. In each letter, he requested that an official public debate be held between him and leading figures of the Buddhist schools. But his appeals were ignored. Instead, the authorities began to view Nichiren and his followers as a threat and contrived to suppress them.

Around that time, the True Word school, which had been holding prayer ceremonies for the defeat of the Mongols, was gaining prestige and influence. Also, a leader of

the True Word Precepts school, the priest Ryokan of Gokuraku-ji temple in Kamakura, had strengthened his ties with government authorities and began to wield significant power. Despite their prominence, Nichiren began to vigorously challenge and refute these erroneous Buddhist schools, which were exerting a negative influence upon the people.

In 1271, Kamakura suffered a severe drought. Ryokan announced that he would conduct a prayer ceremony to bring about rainfall. Hearing of this, Nichiren sent Ryokan a letter containing the following challenge: Should Ryokan succeed in bringing about rain within seven days, Nichiren would become Ryokan's disciple. If no rain were to fall in that seven-day period, however, Ryokan should take faith in the Lotus Sutra.

Ryokan commenced his prayers based on the True Word teachings, but in the course of seven days, not a drop of rain fell. He then requested a seven-day extension, and continued to conduct prayer rituals. Despite all of Ryokan's prayers, not only did no rain fall during that 14-day period, destructive winds struck the city of Kamakura.

Ryokan had clearly lost the challenge. Rather than honestly acknowledging defeat, he grew even more hostile toward Nichiren. Under the name of a priest in his charge, Ryokan filed a lawsuit against the Daishonin. He also appealed to key government authorities as well as to their wives, conspiring to have Nichiren punished.

The public revered Ryokan as a priest of great stature who had mastered the Buddhist teachings. Nichiren, however, saw through Ryokan's benevolent façade and perceived his true nature: that of a priest who had aligned himself with secular power and sought only to fulfill his own ambitions.

On September 10, 1271, Nichiren received a summons from the shogunate. Appearing before the authorities, he was questioned by Hei no Saemon-no-jo Yoritsuna, deputy chief of the office of police and military affairs, second only to the regent himself.

During that encounter, Nichiren remonstrated with Hei no Saemon, instructing him based on Buddhist principles as to the proper attitude and behavior of a ruler who sought to bring peace and security to the people of his nation.

Two days later, on September 12, Hei no Saemon, leading a party of soldiers, stormed Nichiren's dwelling at Matsubagayatsu and arrested him in a manner befitting a rebel or traitor. On that occasion, Nichiren again admonished Hei no Saemon, pointing out that if he should persist in persecuting him, he would be guilty of the crime of toppling the "pillar of Japan" and would invite upon the nation the two calamities of "revolt within one's own domain" and "invasion from foreign lands" predicted in the sutras. This constituted Nichiren's second remonstration with the sovereign.

Without any investigation or questioning, Nichiren was transferred after midnight amid a procession of soldiers to a beach just outside Kamakura called Tatsunokuchi, a place used as an execution ground. Hei no Saemon had secretly and illegally conspired with others to have Nichiren beheaded.

Just as the execution was about to take place, however, a brilliant orb of light (which historians believe to have been a large meteorite or comet fragment) appeared to the north over Enoshima Island and moved across the night sky in a northwesterly direction. This startled and terrified the soldiers guarding Nichiren to the extent that they were unable to follow through with his execution. This series of events is known as the Tatsunokuchi Persecution.

The persecution at Tatsunokuchi constitutes a profoundly significant turning point in Nichiren's lifelong efforts to spread his teachings. That is, at the moment he emerged victorious from this attempt to execute him, he cast off his transient identity as a common mortal and revealed within his life his true identity as the "Buddha of limitless joy from time without beginning." This is referred to as Nichiren "casting off the transient to reveal the true."

From that point on, Nichiren began to fully display the actions of the true Buddha of the Latter Day of the Law, and in that capacity to inscribe the mandala known as the Gohonzon (meaning "object of fundamental respect"— the object of devotion capable of enabling all people to attain Buddhahood).

This article was adapted from the October 2007 Daibyakurenge, *the Soka Gakkai monthly study journal.*

1. The Latter Day of the Law: The name of the age in which the teachings of Shakyamuni Buddha were predicted to lose their power to save the people; that age was thought to begin some 2,000 years after the Buddha's death, and according to views prevalent in Nichiren's time, it had already begun.

2. Three calamities and seven disasters: Catastrophes described in various sutras. The three calamities occur at the end of a *kalpa.* There are two types: the three greater calamities of fire, water and wind, which destroy the world, and the three lesser calamities of high grain prices or inflation (especially that caused by famine), warfare and pestilence, from which human society perishes. The seven disasters include war and natural disasters and are generally held to result from slander of the correct teaching. They are mentioned in the Medicine Master, Benevolent Kings and other sutras. They differ slightly according to the source. Nichiren combined these two different types of calamities in a single phrase to explain the disasters besetting Japan in his time. In his 1260 treatise "On Establishing the Correct Teaching for the Peace of the Land," he states, based on the sutras, that they occur because both the rulers and the populace turn against the correct teaching.

THE LIFE OF
NICHIREN DAISHONIN

This is the conclusion to the article covering Nichiren Daishonin's life. This installment begins with Nichiren's exile to Sado Island and closes with his final days.

THE SADO EXILE

AFTER THE ATTEMPT to execute Nichiren Daishonin on September 12, 1271, at Tatsuno-kuchi failed, the government authorities were uncertain what to do with him. He was taken temporarily to the nearby residence of the deputy constable of Sado Province. Sado, an island off the northeast coast of Japan, was commonly used to exile criminals. Because conditions on the island were so harsh, it was assumed no exiles would survive.

The decision was made to exile Nichiren to Sado Island, and on October 10, 1271, he left the Kamakura region for Sado, arriving on October 28. Nichiren was taken to Tsukahara, a desolate field used for the disposal of abandoned corpses. There, he lived in a small,

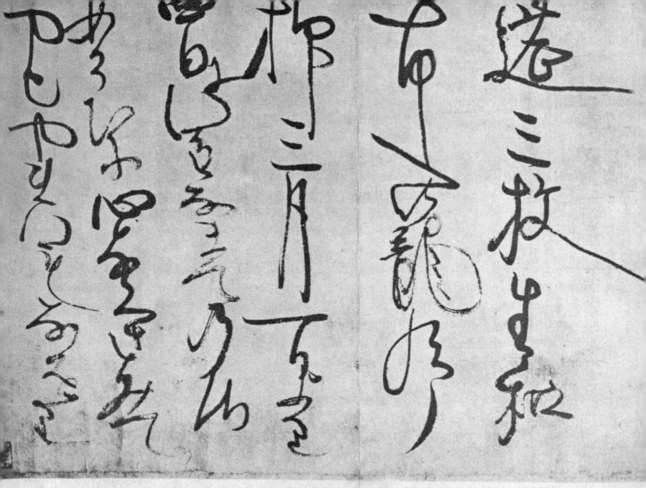

A sample of Nichiren Daishonin's handwritten letter "On the Three Seating Mats" (WND-2, 991).

dilapidated shrine, which had been used for funeral services. He was exposed to bitter cold and lacked sufficient food and clothing. He also was subject to constant threats by Pure Land school believers who bore him great hostility for his condemnation of their distortions of the Buddha's teachings.

At the time, government persecution extended also to Nichiren's followers in Kamakura, some of whom were imprisoned and others driven from their homes or deprived of their land and income. Many disciples, either out of cowardice or the desire to protect themselves or their possessions, came to doubt him and eventually abandoned their faith. Because exile to Sado was tantamount to a death sentence, many believed that their teacher had been defeated after all.

In mid-January 1272, several hundred priests and others representing the major Buddhist schools gathered in front of Nichiren's dwelling to challenge him to a religious debate. Nichiren accepted and easily countered the arguments of each opponent, thoroughly refuting the erroneous doctrines and interpretations they put forth regarding Buddhist teachings.

In February 1272, an insurrection within the ruling Hojo clan caused fighting to erupt in Kamakura and Kyoto. This was significant because Nichiren had predicted civil strife five months earlier. At the time of the Tatsunokuchi Persecution, Nichiren had described the impending calamity of "revolt within one's own domain" to Hei no Saemon-no-jo Yoritsuna.

That summer, Nichiren was moved from Tsukahara to a village called Ichinosawa, affording him a little more comfort and convenience. But the threat to his life posed by hostile believers of other schools did not lessen.

Throughout Nichiren's exile, his disciple Nikko Shonin served his teacher and shared in his hardships.

Among new believers in the Daishonin's teachings were an elderly samurai named Abutsu-bo and his wife, the lay nun Sennichi. Throughout their lives, they played a key role in supporting the Daishonin and the growing community of believers. Their example in faith continues to inspire believers today, more than seven centuries later.

While on Sado, Nichiren produced many important writings, including the particularly significant "The Opening of the Eyes" and "The Object of Devotion for Observing the Mind." "The Opening of the Eyes," written in February 1272, clarifies Nichiren as the true Buddha of the Latter Day of the Law. For this reason, it is known as the writing that reveals the "object of devotion in terms of the Person." "The Object of Devotion for Observing the Mind" clarifies the object of devotion that all people should embrace as the Law of Nam-myoho-renge-kyo. For this reason it is referred to as the writing that reveals the "object of devotion in terms of the Law."

Due in large part to Nichiren's predictions coming true, the government pardoned him from exile in February 1274. The following month, he departed Sado for Kamakura, and the month after that, he again appeared before Hei no Saemon and other officials.

On this occasion, he once again admonished the government for having prayers based on erroneous Buddhist doctrines conducted for the defeat of the Mongol forces. In response to a direct question from Hei no

Saemon, Nichiren predicted that the Mongols would launch an attack against Japan within the year. This encounter would mark his third remonstration with the authorities.

Not long after, a large Mongol force did indeed land on Japan's southernmost main island, Kyushu. With this, the two calamities Nichiren had warned of in his treatise to the government "On Establishing the Correct Teaching for the Peace of the Land"—revolt within one's own domain and invasion from foreign lands—had both occurred, showing his predictions to have been accurate.

As mentioned, the Daishonin had now directly remonstrated with the government concerning these two calamities on three occasions (the first being his submission of "On Establishing the Correct Teaching" to the retired regent Hojo Tokiyori; and the second, his remonstrance to Hei no Saemon during the Tatsunokuchi Persecution). Together, these three warnings are known as Nichiren's "three instances of gaining distinction," deriving from his statement, "Three times now I have gained distinction by having such knowledge" ("The Selection of the Time," *The Writings of Nichiren Daishonin*, vol. 1, p. 579).

Entering Minobu

His three remonstrations with the sovereign having gone unheeded, Nichiren Daishonin left Kamakura for the remote mountain region of Minobu, taking up residence in the province of Kai (present-day Yamanashi Prefecture). The Minobu area was governed by Hakiri Sanenaga (also known as Hakii Sanenaga), the local steward who became a follower of Nichiren after having been converted by Nikko Shonin.

Nichiren entered Minobu in May 1274. In no way did he view this as a retirement or retreat from worldly troubles. While at Minobu, he authored many important writings, including "The Selection of the Time" and "On Repaying Debts of Gratitude," in which he clarified his principal teachings, in particular, the Three Great Secret Laws (the object of devotion of the essential teaching, the sanctuary of the essential teaching and the invocation of the essential teaching). Also, through his lectures on the Lotus Sutra (set down in *The Record of the Orally Transmitted Teachings* and other documents), he focused on educating and training disciples who would bear responsibility for spreading his teachings in the future. During this period, he wrote many personal letters to his lay followers. These letters offered encouragement and instruction in faith and practice to enable each person to become a winner in life and establish the state of supreme enlightenment called Buddhahood. Today, Nichiren's letters and theses are compiled in English in *The Writings of Nichiren Daishonin*, volumes 1 and 2.

THE ATSUHARA PERSECUTION

After Nichiren Daishonin entered Minobu, efforts to spread his teachings progressed particularly in the Fuji area of Suruga Province, southwest of Mount Fuji. Among those converting to Nichiren's teachings were priests and lay believers associated with the Tendai and other Buddhist schools. As a result, the local Tendai temple opposed the propagation efforts of Nichiren's disciples and put pressure on the priests and lay persons who had converted to Nichiren's teachings. This gave rise to incidents involving threats and intimidation toward those who had taken faith in the Mystic Law.

On September 21, 1279, 20 farmers from the Atsuhara area who had taken faith in the Daishonin's teachings were arrested by authorities on false charges and taken to Kamakura.

At the residence of Hei no Saemon, the farmers were harshly interrogated, tortured and threatened with death should they not renounce their faith. Every one of them, however, refused to give in, each standing by his beliefs. In the end, three of the farmers—the brothers Jinshiro, Yagoro and Yarokuro—were put to death, and the remaining 17 were driven from their land.

This and the preceding series of oppressive incidents are collectively known as the Atsuhara Persecution. Observing the courageous spirit and faith of these believers, who refused to compromise even under threat of death, Nichiren sensed that his disciples had now established faith strong enough to endure any kind of persecution while protecting the correct teaching. And so, on October 1, in a letter titled "On Persecutions Befalling the

Sage," Nichiren noted that 27 years had passed since he first declared his teaching and that he had fulfilled the "purpose of my advent" in this world (see WND-1, 996–98). In Buddhism, the "purpose of one's advent" means the objective or purpose for which a Buddha appears in the world.

Then, on October 12, 1279, he established what came to be known as the "Dai-Gohonzon bestowed on Jambudvipa." *Jambudvipa*, here, means the entire world. In inscribing this large Gohonzon, Nichiren Daishonin responded to the powerful faith exhibited by ordinary people in the midst of the Atsuhara Persecution and expressed his deepest wish and vow for kosen-rufu—the propagation of the Law to free all

people from misery and lead them to genuine happiness.

In response to the Atsuhara Persecution, the Daishonin's followers united and fought in the spirit of "many in body, one in mind." Among his followers, a 21-year-old youth, Nanjo Tokimitsu, protected and supported his fellow believers during these trying times.

ENTRUSTING HIS TEACHINGS TO NIKKO SHONIN

In November 1281, Nichiren Daishonin and his disciples completed construction of a permanent priests' lodging at Minobu and

A TIMELINE OF NICHIREN DAISHONIN'S LIFE ❁ ❁ ❁ ❁ ❁ ❁ ❁ ❁

1222 (**Age 1**—at that time in Japan, as soon as a child was born, he or she was considered to be 1 year old)

February 16: Born in Kataumi, Tojo Village, Nagasa District, Awa Province (today, part of Chiba Prefecture)

1253 (**Age 32**)

April 28: Declares the establishment of his teaching at Seicho-ji, a temple in Awa Province

1260 (**Age 39**)

July 16: Submits "On Establishing the Correct Teaching for the Peace of the Land" to retired regent Hojo Tokiyori—his first official remonstration with the sovereign

August 27: Matsubagayatsu Persecution

1261 (**Age 40**)
May 12: Exiled to Izu Peninsula

1264 (**Age 43**)
November 11: Komatsubara Persecution

1268 (**Age 47**)
October 11: Sends 11 letters of remonstration to key figures in Kamakura

1271 (**Age 50**)
September 12: Tatsunokuchi Persecution

October: Begins inscribing the Gohonzon for his disciples

October 10: Sado Exile begins

named it Kuon-ji, *kuon* meaning the "remote past" and *ji* meaning "temple."

In September of the following year, Nichiren entrusted the entirety of the teachings he had expounded and spread throughout his life to Nikko Shonin, charging him with the mission and responsibility of accomplishing kosen-rufu—the widespread propagation of Nam-myoho-renge-kyo.

On September 8, 1282, after consulting his disciples, Nichiren set out from Minobu, where he had lived the previous nine years, and headed toward Hitachi, north of present-day Tokyo, to take advantage of the healing properties of that area's hot springs.

Along the way, he stopped in Ikegami in present-day Tokyo to visit the residence of longtime follower Ikegami Munenaka. There, he made clear his intentions concerning what was to be done after his death.

On September 25, despite the gravity of his illness, he lectured to his followers on his treatise "On Establishing the Correct Teaching for the Peace of the Land." Then on October 13, 1282, Nichiren again declared the entrusting of his teachings to Nikko Shonin, naming him chief priest of Kuon-ji. Later that same day, after 61 years, the noble life of Nichiren Daishonin came to an end.

This article was adapted from the October 2007 Daibyakurenge, *the Soka Gakkai monthly study journal.*

1272 (Age 51)

January 16–17: Tsukahara Debate

February: Revolt breaks out in Kyoto and Kamakura; writes "The Opening of the Eyes"

1273 (Age 52)

April 25: Writes "The Object of Devotion for Observing the Mind"

1274 (Age 53)

March 26: Returns to Kamakura from Sado

April 8: Meets Hei no Saemon; predicts Mongols will attack Japan within the year

May 17: Takes up residence at Mount Minobu

October: Mongol forces invade the southern island of Kyushu (the Bun'ei Invasion)

1279 (Age 58)

September 21: 20 Farmer believers arrested by Shogunate

October 12: Establishes the Dai-Gohonzon

1281 (Age 60)

May 7: Mongols invade Kyushu a second time (the Koan Invasion)

1282 (Age 61)

October 13: Dies at the residence of Ikegami Munenaka at Ikegami in Musashi Province

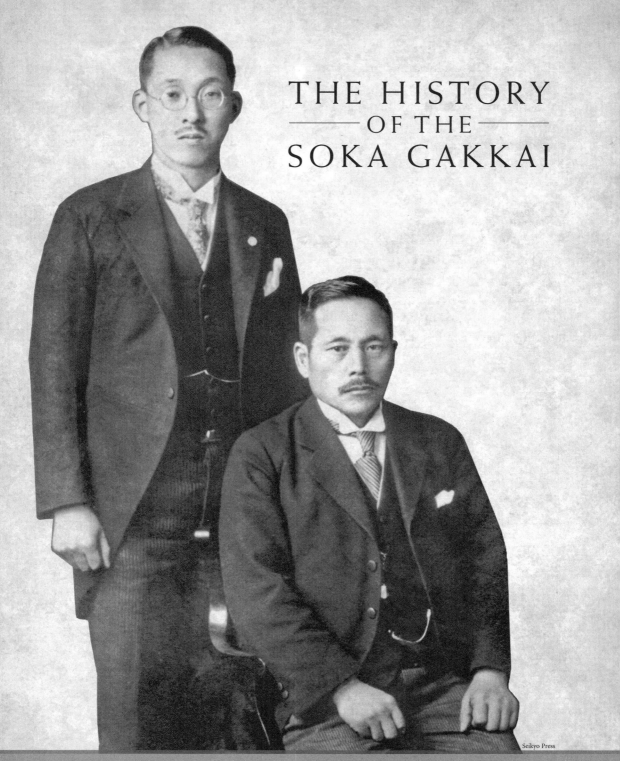

THE HISTORY
OF THE
SOKA GAKKAI

Seikyo Press

Josei Toda (standing) worked with his mentor, Tsunesaburo Makiguchi, for more than 20 years to establish and develop the Soka Kyoiku Gakkai, the precursor of the Soka Gakkai.

THE FOUNDERS OF THE SOKA GAKKAI

THE ORIGIN OF THE SOKA GAKKAI lies in the mentor-and-disciple relationship that existed between first president Tsunesaburo Makiguchi and second president Josei Toda, who were both educators.

Makiguchi was born on June 6, 1871, in Arahama Village in present-day Niigata Prefecture, a small port community on the northwest coast of Japan. He spent much of his youth in Hokkaido where he studied and worked. At 18, he entered the Hokkaido Normal School, a teachers training facility (present-day Hokkaido University of Education). After graduation, he became a teacher at an affiliated elementary school.

Perhaps because he grew up in a small port town that exposed him to the wider world or perhaps because he later spent time in Sapporo, a city that saw rapid modernization, Makiguchi developed a deep interest in geography as a student. As a teacher, he continued to develop his own ideas about how to best teach the subject to students. In 1901, he left Hokkaido for Tokyo to establish his theories. In 1903, he published his first major work, *The Geography of Human Life*, in which he rejects the traditional approach of studying geography through rote memorization and instead offers a systematic and rational approach to education based on the relationship of nature and society to human life.

Until his appointment as principal of Tosei Elementary School in 1913, Makiguchi supported his family by working a variety of jobs in education. He edited educational periodicals and established correspondence courses for young women who did not have access to formal education. He also taught foreign students and developed textbooks for the Ministry of Education.

Meanwhile, Jin'ichi (later known as Josei[1]) Toda was born on February 11, 1900, in Kaga City, in present-day Ishikawa Prefecture. He and his family moved to Atsuta around 1902. After graduating from the senior course at Atsuta Higher Elementary School, he studied independently while also working and eventually obtained a provisional teaching license. In June 1918, Toda became an associate teacher at an elementary school in Yubari, Hokkaido.

Tsunesaburo Makiguchi seriously pursued methods and policies that would assure that disadvantaged children receive equal opportunities in education.

JOSEI TODA ENCOUNTERS HIS MENTOR

Around the beginning of 1920, Toda, who was then 19, visited Tokyo. An acquaintance introduced him to Makiguchi, and the two discussed at length Japan's future as well as educational practice and research. A short while later, Toda moved to Tokyo and gained employment as a substitute teacher at Nishimachi Elementary School, where Makiguchi was principal. Toda decided to work with Makiguchi as his mentor and supported him on a daily basis for the next 23 years.

Between 1913 and 1932, Makiguchi contemplated and refined his educational theories and their practical applications. He was mainly concerned with the happiness of his students. He seriously pursued methods and policies that would assure that disadvantaged children receive equal opportunities in education. He was also an early advocate of community studies in which students learn and appreciate the various aspects of their local communities.

During his efforts to solidify his educational approach, Makiguchi encountered Nichiren Buddhism. The teachings of Nichiren Daishonin resonated deeply with Makiguchi's ideals, and he found no contradictions between the tenets of Nichiren Buddhism and his scientific and rational approach to education. In 1928, when Makiguchi was 57, he converted to Nichiren Buddhism. Toda followed suit.

THE FOUNDING OF THE VALUE-CREATING EDUCATION SOCIETY

After encountering Makiguchi, Toda followed his mentor from Nishimachi to Mikasa Elementary School. Then, when Makiguchi was transferred to his next school, Toda decided to end his career as an elementary school teacher and, in 1923, established Jishu Gakkan, a private school for elementary students studying for the competitive entrance examination for secondary-level education. This private school also offered Makiguchi a place to freely pursue his research and develop his educational theories.

Determined to realize his mentor's goal of publishing his educational theory, Toda gave his full-fledged support in editing and organizing Makiguchi's copious notes from his many years of educational research, application and experience. Toda also invested his own funds in the publication of his mentor's work.

On November 18, 1930, with Toda's dedicated assistance, Makiguchi published the first volume of *Soka kyoikugaku taikei*, or *The System of Value-Creating Pedagogy*. The copyright page includes the names of Tsunesaburo Makiguchi, the author, and Josei Toda, the publisher, and the publishing entity is listed as "Soka Kyoiku Gakkai" (Value-Creating Education Society)—the predecessor of the Soka Gakkai (Value Creation Society). Thus, November 18 of that year is regarded as the day of the Soka Gakkai's founding.

In the title of his work, Makiguchi uses the word *soka*, which means *value creation*. The term derived from a discussion between Toda and Makiguchi. Thus, *The System of Value-Creating Pedagogy* was a work that crystallized the oneness of mentor and disciple. *Soka* encompasses Makiguchi's idea that the purpose of education and of life is to pursue happiness, and in order to do that, one must create value in life. He writes: "We begin with the recognition that humans cannot create matter. We can, however, create value. Creating value is, in fact, our very humanity. When we praise persons for their 'strength of character,' we are really acknowledging their superior ability to create value."[2]

PRACTICING NICHIREN BUDDHISM

In 1937, the Soka Kyoiku Gakkai began meeting regularly as an organization of educators who supported the theory of Soka education. But it quickly extended membership to non-educators as well and developed into an organization of people from all walks of life interested in how the teachings and philosophy of Nichiren Daishonin could help transform Japanese society at that time.

Eventually, the Soka Kyoiku Gakkai became a lay practitioner society of the Nichiren Shoshu school, but it operated very differently from other lay organizations. Instead of depending on priests, Makiguchi and Toda took full responsibility for running all meetings and giving guidance in faith. The Soka Gakkai was, from its very beginning, an organization of lay believers not restricted by the traditions of the priesthood.

Seikyo Press

Josei Toda works while studying to become certified as a teacher, 1917.

Since its inception, the Buddhist practice of Soka Gakkai members has been based on the original intent of Nichiren Daishonin and of Buddhism itself, focusing on helping people realize happiness through practice and faith, and striving for peace and prosperity in society. Throughout the 1930s and early 1940s, the Soka Kyoiku Gakkai grew steadily, peaking at 3,000 members during the early 1940s as propagation and discussion meetings developed in urban and rural areas throughout Japan. Activities centered on small gatherings in members' homes, as well as occasional larger meetings in public venues.

Tsunesaburo Makiguchi (second row, center) with fellow Taisho Elementary School teachers, 1919.

A BATTLE AGAINST MILITARISM

In the mid-1930s, the Japanese government began restricting many aspects of life as a way to enforce support of its war effort. To form spiritual unity among citizens, the militarist authorities increasingly incorporated state Shinto religious practices in state functions and endorsed the religion as its spiritual pillar. By the early 1940s, the government intensified its efforts. Makiguchi's and Toda's religious activities attracted the attention of the government's Special Higher Police, which kept Soka Gakkai discussion meetings under surveillance. Their refusal to compromise the humane principles of Nichiren Buddhism and promote the nationalistic beliefs of Shintoism had caused them to be labeled as a threat.

By 1943, citizens were required to worship a Shinto talisman. In June that year,

Nichiren Shoshu priests who feared government authorities instructed members of the Soka Gakkai to accept the Shinto talisman. The priests' attitudes directly contradicted the intent of Nichiren Daishonin and Nikko Shonin. In contrast, the Soka Gakkai leaders refused to accept the talisman; they continued to uphold their belief in Nam-myoho-renge-kyo despite the mounting pressures.

As a result, on July 6, 1943, Makiguchi, who was in his 70s, was arrested while attending a discussion meeting in Izu. On the same day, Toda was arrested in Tokyo, along with 21 leaders of the Soka Kyoiku Gakkai. They were charged with blasphemy and for violation of the Peace Preservation Law, which targeted any form of dissent against the government. Only Makiguchi and Toda maintained their faith throughout the intense interrogation and never recanted their beliefs. Makiguchi and Toda were confined to prison.

President Toda's "Religious Awakening"

In prison, Makiguchi continued to share Nichiren Buddhism, even with the prosecutors and judges who questioned him during his imprisonment. He never submitted to the demands of the authorities, upholding his conviction in Buddhism with his entire being.

Toda's greatest concern was for his elderly mentor. He prayed fervently: "I'm still young. My mentor is seventy-three. Please, if they'll release him even one day sooner, let me take the blame for both of us."[3]

From early 1944, Toda chanted Nammyoho-renge-kyo in his jail cell and studied the Lotus Sutra. Through intense contemplation, he came to the realization that Buddha is life itself.

In November, after chanting more vigorously than ever, he awakened to the truth that he himself was among the Bodhisattvas of the Earth, who at the Ceremony in the Air were entrusted with the mission of accomplishing kosen-rufu after Shakyamuni's passing.

On November 18, 1944, Makiguchi passed away in the Tokyo Detention House. He had died of malnutrition at the age of 73. His death coincides with the anniversary of the Soka Kyoiku Gakkai's founding. Makiguchi lived in accord with Nichiren Daishonin's teachings, dedicated to the revival of Nichiren's spirit to save all people from suffering by propagating the Mystic Law. He never succumbed to any force attempting to make him stray from that path.

His disciple, Toda, through the enlightenment he experienced in prison, awakened to his true mission as a leader of kosen-rufu. This religious awakening became the starting point for the development of the Soka Gakkai in the postwar era.

After the war, Toda expressed the following at Makiguchi's memorial in 1946:

> *In your vast and boundless compassion, you let me accompany you even to prison. As a result, I could read with my entire being the passage from the Lotus Sutra, "those persons who had heard the Law / dwelled here and there in various Buddha lands, / constantly reborn in company with their teachers."[4] The benefit of this was coming to know the essential purpose of a Bodhisattva of the Earth, and to absorb with my very life even a small degree of the sutra's meaning. Could there be any greater happiness than this?[5]*

"Those persons . . . reborn in company with their teachers" is a passage from the seventh chapter of the Lotus Sutra. These words signify the deep bond between mentor and disciple, always reborn together to fight for the happiness of humanity. Josei Toda's words express his deep sense of gratitude toward his mentor, Tsunesaburo Makiguchi.

This article was adapted from the October 2007 Daibyakurenge, the Soka Gakkai's monthly study journal.

1. Toda changed his name twice—first during his late teens to Jogai, literally meaning "outside the castle," and later to Josei, or "castle sage."
2. Tsunesaburo Makiguchi, *Education for Creative Living*, edited by Dayle M. Bethel and translated by Alfred Birnbaum (Ames, Iowa: Iowa State University Press, 1994), pp. 5–6.
3. *The Human Revolution*, p. 90.
4. *The Lotus Sutra*, p. 140.
5. *The Human Revolution*, p. 1967.

THE HISTORY
OF THE
SOKA GAKKAI

Seikyo Press

Daisaku Ikeda (left) and second Soka Gakkai president Josei Toda
playing drums at a commemorative festival, Japan, 1956.

THE DEVELOPMENT OF THE SOKA GAKKAI IN POSTWAR JAPAN

JOSEI TODA was released from prison on July 3, 1945. Physically frail, he burned with a fierce resolve to rebuild the Soka Kyoiku Gakkai (Value-Creating Education Society), which had been virtually dissolved during World War II.

At the beginning of 1946, Toda began lecturing on the Lotus Sutra, and he had also resumed holding discussion meetings and began propagation efforts in rural areas. He renamed the organization the Soka Gakkai (Value Creation Society), reflecting a commitment to the broader goal of kosen-rufu, which is, in essence, the process of spreading the principles of Nichiren Buddhism throughout society for the lasting peace and happiness of all people.

In 1947, Toda met Daisaku Ikeda at a discussion meeting.

DAISAKU IKEDA'S EARLY YEARS

Daisaku Ikeda was born on January 2, 1928, in present-day Oomorikita in Ota Ward, Tokyo. The Pacific War broke out when he was 13. As the battlefront situation worsened, his four older brothers were drafted. Though struggling with tuberculosis, young Daisaku supported his family by working at a munitions factory.

Daisaku was made painfully aware of the tragedies of war. The Ikeda family lost two homes in air raids. When his eldest brother, Kiichi, came home on leave, he shared accounts of the tremendous suffering inflicted upon the common people during the war. The stories of cruelty and inhumanity deeply saddened and angered Daisaku, and the pain deepened when he later learned that Kiichi had died in battle.

After the war, Ikeda turned his attention to philosophy and literature in search for meaning amid the pain and chaos of daily life in postwar Japan. He writes: "I was 17 when World War II ended. There was among young people a tormented sense of spiritual void. It wasn't just the physical landscape that had been reduced to ashes. The bizarre system of values drilled into us in the wartime years had been exposed as fraudulent and razed to the ground" (*Embracing the Future*, p. 14).

During this period of sorrow and philosophical inquiry, he attended his first Soka Gakkai discussion meeting on August 14, 1947. At that meeting, Josei Toda lectured on Nichiren Daishonin's well-known writing "On Establishing the Correct Teaching for the Peace of the Land" (see *The Writings of Nichiren Daishonin*, vol. 1, pp. 6–32).

When Ikeda was introduced to Toda toward the end of the meeting, he posed the following four questions: "What is a correct way of life?"; "What is a true patriot?"; "What is Nam-myoho-renge-kyo?"; and "What is your opinion of the emperor?" Toda's answers were to the point, logical and without pretense, and they expressed an underlying conviction. *How succinctly he answers!* Ikeda thought. *There is no confusion in him. I think I can believe and follow this man* (see *The Human Revolution*, p. 232).

Though it was only his first encounter with Toda, Ikeda felt very close to him. And he respected the fact that Toda had been imprisoned for his refusal to compromise his religious beliefs in the face of pressure from Japan's militarist government. As their dialogue concluded, he asked if he could study

Seikyo Press

Daisaku Ikeda works as editor of a youth magazine at the Nihon Shogakkan, Josei Toda's publishing company, 1949.

under Toda (see *The Human Revolution*, pp. 224–32).

Ten days later, on August 24, he joined the Soka Gakkai, vowing to follow Toda as his mentor.

Ikeda went on to deepen his understanding of Buddhism through attending Toda's lectures on the Lotus Sutra. In January 1949, he was hired at Toda's publishing company as the editor of a youth magazine.

Daisaku Ikeda Fully Supports His Mentor

In July 1949, the Soka Gakkai launched its study magazine on Nichiren Buddhism, *The Daibyakurenge*. For the inaugural issue, Josei Toda wrote "The Philosophy of Life," a thesis in which he discussed the Buddhist view of life and death.

Later that same year, the postwar economy worsened and the publishing company fell upon hard financial times. The youth magazine Daisaku Ikeda edited was suspended. Despite this setback, Ikeda quickly switched gears to devote himself fully to building up Toda's credit association. He gave everything to support his mentor in business and private matters.

In 1950, the disorder in the economy intensified, and Toda's entrepreneurial efforts were seriously impaired. Though Toda's businesses had financed the initial growth of the Soka Gakkai, as his enterprises faltered and his debt grew, some members—especially those connected to his unsuccessful credit association—lost confidence in him and the Soka Gakkai. To avoid burdening the organization with his financial struggles, on August 24, Toda resigned as general director of the Soka Gakkai.

With this, a worried Ikeda asked Toda whether the new general director would become his mentor.

Toda replied: "No … I am your mentor, although I cause so much trouble for you all the time" (*The Human Revolution*, p. 510).

One by one, employees of Toda's company left, but Toda remained steadfast, devoting his entire being to repaying the company's massive debt. Ikeda fervently supported him throughout, even quitting night school, determined to help get Toda financially solvent and to see him become president of the Soka Gakkai. Toda took it upon himself to educate his young disciple by conducting private tutoring sessions spanning a variety of academic interests. "Toda University" continued until Toda's death.

Despite the challenges they faced, Toda shared his vision for the future with Ikeda. His goals ranged from starting a newspaper for kosen-rufu to founding a university. In time, both the *Seikyo Shimbun* (inaugurated in 1951) and Soka University (established in 1971) emerged as the fruit of their joint efforts.

Josei Toda took it upon himself to educate his young disciple by conducting private tutoring sessions spanning a variety of academic interests. "Toda University" continued until Mr. Toda's death.

Daisaku Ikeda leads a song as the Soka Gakkai youth division leader as second Soka Gakkai president Josei Toda (back, right) looks on, 1954.

Josei Toda Becomes Second President of the Soka Gakkai

Josei Toda and Daisaku Ikeda struggled intensely between 1950 and 1951 to turn Toda's financial situation around. After much reflection, Toda determined: "Whatever hardship may befall me, I must put it aside. This I will not do for my own sake but for the cause of fulfilling my mission. I must not by any means leave even a single teaching of Nichiren Daishonin's unfulfilled" (*The Human Revolution*, p. 529).

During this tumultuous time, Ikeda made all-out efforts to fulfill his deepest wish—that his mentor be freed from his constricting financial situation in order to become president of the Soka Gakkai and assume full leadership of kosen-rufu.

Within a year, Toda's financial difficulties were behind him. Not only had it been a harsh year of surmounting financial problems, the two had also suffered major health setbacks.

This period of time is described in *The Human Revolution* as follows: "It can well be said that the behind-the-scenes stories of these two men during that period were the deciding factors of the Soka Gakkai's development and existence today. The Soka Gakkai's marvelous development after Toda's inauguration as second president in 1951, its leaping advance after his death and many other realities can only be attributed to the fostering of that decisive seed during this trial period, as well as, of course, the supremacy of Nichiren Daishonin's Buddhism" (pp. 539–40).

On May 3, 1951, Josei Toda was inaugurated as second Soka Gakkai president. During his inaugural address, he vowed to accomplish a membership of 750,000 households at a time when Soka Gakkai members numbered approximately 3,000. Many in attendance had difficulty fathoming how his goal would be achieved. Toda, however, had already begun preparations for a widespread propagation movement and was so confident of success that he told the members, "If my goal should not be attained by the end of my life, you need not hold a funeral for me, but just throw my remains into the sea off Shinagawa, all right?" (*The Human Revolution*, p. 563).

Just prior to becoming president, on April 20, Toda launched the *Seikyo Shimbun*, a daily newspaper for Soka Gakkai members. His novel *The Human Revolution*, which covered the early development of the Soka Gakkai, began as a series in the first issue of the newspaper.

Soon after his inauguration, Toda formed the women's division on June 10, the young men's division on July 11 and the young women's division on July 19.

In January 1952, Toda assigned Ikeda responsibility for Kamata Chapter. The following month, the membership in Kamata Chapter increased by an unprecedented 201 member-households.

With the organization steadily growing, Toda firmly believed that diligent and correct study of Nichiren's writings was indispensable for the progress of kosen-rufu. He commissioned Nichiren Buddhist scholar Nichiko Hori to compile a collection of all of Nichiren's available writings. *Gosho zenshu* (The Collected Writings of Nichiren Daishonin) was published in April 1952, marking the 700th anniversary of the establishment of Nichiren's teachings. As a result, a thorough grounding in Nichiren's writings became the foundation of Soka Gakkai members' practice.

In September, the Japanese government formally recognized the Soka Gakkai as a religious organization.

Ikeda, in the meantime, was appointed to take on various responsibilities in the organization. In January 1953, he became the leader of the young men's division First Corps, and in April, he was appointed acting Bunkyo Chapter leader. The following March, he became the Soka Gakkai youth division leader.

STRUGGLES WITH AUTHORITY

Nichiren Daishonin's determination to establish "the correct teaching for the peace of the land" encapsulated his lifelong battle for the happiness of all people and realizing peace in society. With that same spirit, and to confront corruption in politics, the Soka Gakkai for the first time endorsed candidates for the national parliament in April 1955.

The following year, Daisaku Ikeda led propagation efforts in the Kansai region, which resulted in Osaka Chapter growing by an unprecedented 11,111 member-households in the single month of May. In July, Ikeda was put in charge of the Soka Gakkai election effort in Osaka.

Three candidates won seats in the national elections, causing the Soka Gakkai to now be considered an influential organization. At the same time, the Soka Gakkai faced opposition from various groups threatened by its success.

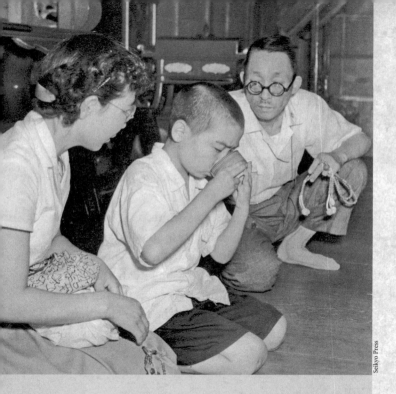

Seikyo Press

With the organization steadily growing, Josei Toda firmly believed that diligent and correct study of Nichiren's writings was indispensable for the progress of kosen-rufu.

Second Soka Gakkai president Josei Toda encourages members, 1956.

For example, in June 1957, Ikeda went to Hokkaido where the Yubari branch of the Japan Coal Miners Union had attempted to oppress and intimidate local coal miners who belonged to the Soka Gakkai. He firmly protested such treatment and took action through debate and dialogue to resolve the problem.

Immediately after this, on July 3, 1957, the Osaka police arrested and detained Ikeda, falsely charging him with election fraud based on violation of election laws, actually committed by other Soka Gakkai members.

Ikeda was interrogated for 15 days, and prosecutors threatened that if he did not admit his guilt, they were going to arrest Toda. At the time, Toda was extremely weak, his health failing, and Ikeda could not bear the thought

of Toda returning to jail. To protect his mentor, Ikeda conceded and took the entire blame upon himself. On July 17, he was indicted and released from the Osaka Detention Center. Ikeda battled in court for more than four years, and on January 15, 1962, he emerged victorious, cleared of all charges.

ENTRUSTING THE FUTURE OF KOSEN-RUFU TO THE YOUTH

On September 8, 1957, Josei Toda passionately and publicly condemned all use of nuclear weapons, calling for their immediate abolition. Based on the devastating destructiveness, the

Second Soka Gakkai president Josei Toda delivers his Declaration for the Abolition of Nuclear Weapons, Japan, September 8, 1957.

total disregard for all life and the horrible aftermath that accompanies the use of nuclear weapons, Toda denounced those who used them as the embodiment of "evil incarnate." This declaration set the tone for the Soka Gakkai's future peace movement (see *The Human Revolution*, pp. 485–87).

In December, the organization's membership reached 750,000 households—Toda's ultimate goal. In March 1958, the Grand Lecture Hall, donated by the Soka Gakkai, was completed at the head temple, Taiseki-ji. On March 16, an historic meeting took place in which 6,000 youth assembled from throughout Japan at the head temple. At this gathering, Toda passed the responsibility for accomplishing kosen-rufu to the youth, and he declared, "The Soka Gakkai is the king of the religious world!" March 16 is celebrated today as Kosen-rufu Day.

On April 2, roughly two weeks following that ceremony, Toda died at age 58. Having drawn upon his enlightenment in prison as a source of strength, he had succeeded in rebuilding the Soka Gakkai and creating a solid foundation for kosen-rufu. His legacy includes the numerous successors he raised, among them the future third president of the Soka Gakkai, his closest disciple, Daisaku Ikeda.

This article was adapted from the October 2007 Daibyakurenge, the Soka Gakkai's monthly study journal.

THE HISTORY
—OF THE—
SOKA GAKKAI

Seikyo Shimbun

Daisaku Ikeda leads a song, April 1973.

DAISAKU IKEDA: ESTABLISHING A NETWORK OF BUDDHIST HUMANISM THROUGHOUT THE WORLD

ON MAY 3, 1960, WHEN DAISAKU IKEDA was inaugurated as the third president of the Soka Gakkai, he declared: "Though I am young, from this day I will take leadership as a representative of President Toda's disciples and advance with you another step toward the substantive realization of kosen-rufu" (*The Human Revolution*, p. 1971).

Determined to fulfill second Soka Gakkai president Josei Toda's wish to spread Nichiren Buddhism worldwide, on October 2, 1960, five months after his inauguration, Ikeda set out to visit nine cities in North and South America. Wherever he went, he encouraged the Soka Gakkai members, many of whom were Japanese immigrant laborers or women who had married American military men and relocated to the United States.

In New York, Ikeda and his party visited the United Nations headquarters. Here, Ikeda contemplated the role and potential of that international body in creating peace in the world. This subject became a sustained focus of his attention—an issue he continues to explore through proposals, dialogues and various collaborative efforts between the SGI and the United Nations. Since 1981, the SGI has been a nongovernmental organization affiliated with the United Nations. The organization has been active in public education with a focus on peace, disarmament, human rights and sustainable development, as well as providing humanitarian assistance and promoting interfaith dialogue.

In January 1961, he made goodwill visits to Asia, including to Hong Kong and India. During the trip, and particularly during a visit to Bodh Gaya—the site in India traditionally regarded as the place where Shakyamuni attained enlightenment—he pondered the idea of creating an institution dedicated to research into Asian philosophy and culture as a means of promoting dialogue and peace. The following year, he established the Institute of Oriental Philosophy in Tokyo.

In 1963, he founded the Min-On Concert Association, dedicated to fostering peace through cultural and artistic exchange. He writes: "Cultured people value peace and lead others to a world of beauty, hope and bright tomorrows. Tyrannical authority, on the other hand, only leads people to darkness—the opposite of art.

"For that reason, nurturing and spreading an appreciation for art and culture are crucial in creating peace" (*Discussions on Youth*, second edition, p. 169).

Ikeda also traveled extensively throughout Japan to encourage Soka Gakkai members. He especially focused on raising the next generation of leaders, conducting lectures on the works of Nichiren Daishonin for representatives of the student division. In June 1964, the high school division was created and in 1965, the junior high school and elementary school divisions were established.

In 1965, he began writing his serialized novel *The Human Revolution*, which details Toda's struggle to reconstruct the Soka Gakkai after his release from prison at the end of World War II. This and its ongoing sequel, *The New Human Revolution*, chronicle the history of the Soka Gakkai spanning 80 years.

Seikyo Pr

Daisaku Ikeda talks with South African poet Oswald M. Mtshali (right), May 1991.

FORGING PEACE THROUGH DIALOGUE

In an effort to create different pathways to peace, Daisaku Ikeda often exchanges views with representatives of cultural, political, educational and artistic fields from around the world. The number of formal encounters of this kind has been estimated at 1,600. One of his early dialogues was with the Austrian intellectual and proponent of European unity Count Richard Coudenhove-Kalergi in 1967. Their exchange was published in 1972 in Japanese under the title *Bunmei: nishi to higashi* (Civilization: East and West). *Choose*

Life, Ikeda's best-known dialogue, covers a two-and-a-half-year discussion (in person and through correspondence) with eminent British historian Arnold J. Toynbee. Ikeda's relationship with Dr. Toynbee opened many doors for further dialogues with other notable thinkers.

He has also published dialogues with former Soviet president Mikhail Gorbachev, Nobel Peace prize-winning scientists and peace activists Linus Pauling and Joseph Rotblat, futurist Hazel Henderson and many others.

During the 1970s, following a visit to China where he saw the people of the country living in fear of Soviet attack, Ikeda engaged in a series of intensive dialogues with political figures of leading Cold War countries. He writes:

In 1974, 35 years ago, I visited China and the Soviet Union, which were then in a state of considerable tension. In Japan, a storm of criticism descended upon me. Failing to understand my motives, many questioned my traveling to nations that rejected religion. Nevertheless, I met and spoke with innumerable ordinary citizens in China and the Soviet Union, forging bonds of friendship. For it was my firm belief that amicable exchange among the people of the world, transcending all differences, is the way to build an unshakable foundation for peace. I also engaged in frank discussions with the leaders of both nations.

The following year, in January 1975, I flew to the United States and also had meaningful dialogues with leaders there who held the keys to peace.

That very month, the SGI was founded on Guam, the final stop on my U.S. visit. In other words, the SGI was established in the midst of my efforts to bring the United States, China and the Soviet Union closer together through dialogue in a world shrouded by the dark clouds of the Cold War.

History teaches us the bitter lesson that coercive balances of power and attempts to resolve conflicts through military force only create greater division. Choosing dialogue is the key to building peace and achieving a victory of our inner humanity.

Since the founding of the SGI, this truth has continued to ring out vibrantly across the globe as the cry of world citizens.

(January 1, 2009, *World Tribune*, p. 4)

In 1983, Ikeda wrote his first peace proposal to the United Nations, offering a perspective on issues such as nuclear abolition, the environment and strengthening the United Nations. Since then, he has submitted a peace proposal each year on January 26, commemorating the day in 1975 when the SGI was established.

SEPARATION FROM NICHIREN SHOSHU

The Soka Gakkai, from the time of its inception in 1930, was the primary benefactor of the Nichiren Shoshu priesthood. The Soka Gakkai's growth after World War II transformed Nichiren Shoshu from a fairly obscure Buddhist school into one of the largest religious bodies in Japan.

As the Soka Gakkai membership grew during the 1970s, Daisaku Ikeda began to assert in his speeches and lectures that from the perspective of Nichiren's writings, lay believers should in no way be considered inferior to the priesthood. His actions were prompted by increasing reports of priests acting in an authoritarian and abusive manner toward the laity. Lay members complained of feeling accelerating pressure to offer alms to the priests while, at the same time, being treated disparagingly. Ikeda tried to engage the priests in dialogue about these concerns.

Many priests felt threatened by Ikeda's public assertions and his considerable influence with the membership. Opportunists within the Soka Gakkai attempted to undermine Ikeda by exploiting these fears, feeding the priests alarming but false reports about the Soka Gakkai's supposed ill intentions. Tensions grew in a climate of accusation and counteraccusation.

In an essay about that intense period, Ikeda writes:

SGI President and Mrs. Ikeda meet with master Chinese painter and calligrapher Fang Zhaoling (center) in Hong Kong, December 2000.

To protect my sincere fellow members, I sought with all my being to find a way to forge harmonious unity between the priesthood and lay believers. But all my efforts looked as if they would come to naught when a top Soka Gakkai leader—who later quit and renounced his faith—made inappropriate remarks. The Gakkai's enemies, who were waiting all along to destroy us, pounced eagerly. The priests raised an uproar and demanded that I take responsibility for this person's words.

I agonized over the situation. I knew I had to prevent further suffering from being inflicted on our members and to protect them from the persecution of the priests. Mr. Toda had said that the Soka Gakkai was more precious to him than his own life. The Gakkai is an organization that follows the Buddha's intent and decree to the letter; it is dedicated to the happiness of the people, the propagation of Buddhism and world peace.

My resolve to take all the blame upon myself and to resign the presidency gradually grew firm within me.

(May 14, 1999, *World Tribune*, p. 7)

When Ikeda declared his intention to step down, the conditions set by the priesthood for conciliation were harsh. Ikeda was forbidden from addressing the Soka Gakkai members at the organization's gatherings; his writings were not to appear in the organization's publications.

Ikeda stepped down as president on April 24, 1979. Restricted from publishing his guidance, he wrote short poems and calligraphic works for individual members. Unable to speak publicly, he traveled throughout the country, visiting members in their homes to offer them personal encouragement. Ikeda took what had seemed a debilitating setback as an opportunity to fulfill an even grander vision—to fortify the SGI and its mission to establish a solid network for building peace throughout the world.

The conflict between the Soka Gakkai and the priesthood was eventually settled. Later, Ikeda again fulfilled a more public profile in Japan as a Buddhist leader.

During the next 10 years, however, Nikken Abe, as high priest, conspired either to disband the Soka Gakkai or bring it under direct control of the priesthood. The same ex-Soka Gakkai leaders who had earlier orchestrated Ikeda's resignation colluded with Nikken toward this end.

After compiling a list of complaints against the lay organization, the priesthood excommunicated the entire Soka Gakkai organization in November 1991. Despite repeated requests from the Soka Gakkai, Nikken refused to meet with Ikeda for dialogue.

Following notice of excommunication, a small percentage of SGI members chose to follow the priesthood. The vast majority, however, remained with the SGI, viewing the excommunication as a liberation from an archaic institution, giving the organization the freedom to pursue a more modern and enlightened approach for applying Nichiren Buddhism to the conditions of modern global society.

BUILDING AN EVERLASTING FOUNDATION FOR PEACE

Daisaku Ikeda, now 81, continues to pursue dialogue with philosophers, scientists and world leaders, as well as submitting annual peace proposals to the United Nations. He has been acknowledged by numerous institutions, governments and organizations as a true builder of peace.

Still today, he prepares and delivers addresses at monthly Soka Gakkai leaders meetings to encourage people throughout the world to continue developing and strengthening their lives so that they may establish happiness in their own lives and peace in their communities.

Among his many endeavors, he continues writing daily installments of *The New Human Revolution*, as well as two ongoing study series—the "Writings of Nichiren Daishonin and the Oneness of Mentor and Disciple," serialized in the *World Tribune*, and "Learning From the Writings of Nichiren Daishonin: The Teachings for Victory," which commences in English in this issue of *Living Buddhism*.

Now, more than anything, he is putting his energy into encouraging youth around the world to take on the same struggle and challenge as he, to build an everlasting foundation for peace in the world.

For the more than 62 years since beginning his practice of Nichiren Buddhism, Ikeda has kept the guidance and vision of his mentor, Josei Toda, close to his heart. He says: "Mr. Toda was focused on the world. He was thinking about humanity as a whole. He once said earnestly: 'Nichiren Buddhism is like the light of the sun. By embracing faith in the Mystic Law, countless Soka Gakkai members have risen up from the depths of despair and vibrantly revitalized their lives.' The Mystic Law makes it possible for humankind to transform its karma. It is here that we find the mission of the Soka Gakkai, an organization dedicated to building peace" (March 20, 2009, *World Tribune*, p. 4).

Adapted from daisakuikeda.org and the October 2007 Daibyakurenge, the Soka Gakkai's monthly study journal.

INDEX

A

Abutsu-bo, 62
Ajatashatru, 20; transformation of, 23
Ananda, 19, 21; "This is what I heard," 23
Aniruddha, 19
Ashoka, transformation of, 24
Atsuhara Persecution, 63–64; "many in body, one in mind," 64

B

Bimbisara, 20
bodhisattva(s), 25, 30, 34, 38
Bodhisattvas of the Earth, 71
Buddhahood, 11, 14, 20, 26, 31, 34, 38, 39, 41, 42, 43, 46, 51, 59, 63
Buddha(s), 7, 9; appearance of, 8, 29; nature, 9, 11, 20, 25, 39, 42–43; vow of, 5. *See also* Nichiren Daishonin
Buddhism, 7, 11, 29; to attain unsurpassed enlightenment, 7; beginning of, 17; and confronting errors, 8; during Meiji period, 48; First Buddhist Council, 23–24, 26; internal way, 7; and native belief systems, 31; purpose of one's advent in, 64; schisms in, 24–25; Second Buddhist Council, 24; the sufferings of birth and death endured since time without beginning, 7
Buddhist humanism, Daisaku Ikeda on, 6–9

C

chanting, self-reflection aspect of, 43
Chinese Buddhism, 29–34, 37–38
Choose Life (Toynbee), 82
compassion, 7, 8, 9, 11, 15, 20, 25, 29, 51, 54, 71
conduct (behavior), 8
Coudenhove-Kalergi, Count Richard, *Bunmei: nishi to higashi* (Civilization: East and West), 82
courage, 14, 43, 46, 51, 63

D

The Daibyakurenge, 75
Daosheng, 32
delusion, 14–15
Dengyo, and Tendai school, 38–39
dependent origination, 42
determination, 8
Devadatta, 19, 23; symbolizes, 20
Dewey, John, 48
dialogue, 17, 83; Daisaku Ikeda's use of, 50, 51, 78, 81, 82–83, 85; Tsunesaburo Makiguchi's use of, 51
disciples, of Kumarajiva, 32; mission of, 8–9; of Nichiren Daishonin, 45, 46, 58, 61, 62, 63, 64, 65; of Shakyamuni, 17, 18–19, 20, 21
discussion meeting(s), 17; under surveillance by militarist authorities, 70
disunity, 20
Dogen, 40
Dozen-bo, 56

Nichimoku Shonin, 46
Nichiren Buddhism, 8–9, 15, 40–43, 49–50, 85; essence of, 41–42; growth of, 51; principle of "establishing the correct teaching for the peace of the land" in, 43
Nichiren Daishonin, 9, 14, 18, 20, 26–27, 34, 39, 41–42, 50; *See also* Buddha; aim of, 46; "to become the wisest person in Japan," 55; Buddha of limitless joy from time without beginning, 59; and Buddhahood, 63; casting off the transient to reveal the true, 59; the correct teaching for the peace of the land, 77; death of, 45, 65; declaration of, 40, 56; "On Establishing the Correct Teaching for the Peace of the Land," 57–58, 62, 65; invasion of foreign lands, 57, 58, 59, 62; Izu Exile of, 57; receiving a "jewel" of wisdom, 40, 55; Komatsubara Persecution of, 57–58; and Kuon-ji, 64–65; life of, 40, 54–65; and the Lotus Sutra, 56; Lotus Sutra lectures in *The Record of the Orally Transmitted Teachings* of, 63; in Minobu, 62–63; mission of, 54, 56; and the Mystic Law, 56; "The Object of Devotion for Observing the Mind," 62; "The Opening of the Eyes," 62; "On Persecutions Befalling the Sage," 63–64; pillar of Japan, 59; purpose of advent of, 64; remonstration by, 57, 59, 62; "On Repaying Debts of Gratitude," 63; revolt with one's own domain, 57, 59, 61, 62; Sado Exile of, 60–62; "The Selection of the Time," 63; studies at Jisso-ji temple, 56–57; three instances of gaining distinction, 62; writings of, 63, 76

Nichiren Shoshu school, Soka Gakkai members' contribution to, 49–50
Nikken Abe, 85; scheme of, 50
Niko, slander of, 45–46
Nikko Shonin, 48, 57, 62; death of, 46; great guide and teacher in the spread of the essential teaching, 45; and kosen-rufu, 65; Omosu Seminary, 46; as superintendent of Kuon-ji, 45; *The Twenty-six Admonitions of*, 46
Nissei, slander of, 48

P
Pauling, Linus, 82
peace, 7, 9, 11, 32, 43, 51, 57, 59, 69, 73, 77, 79; foundation for, 82, 83, 84, 85
peace and security, 43
Precepts school, 40–42, 58
priests, 48–49; Nichikan on, 47
Pure Land school, 40, 42, 56
Purna, 24

R
Rahula, 12
Rotblat, Joseph, 82
Ryokan, Nichiren challenges, 58

S
Saicho. *See* Dengyo
self, establishing the, 21
Sengrui, and the Lotus Sutra, 32
Sennichi, the lay nun, 62
Shakyamuni, 7, 8, 26, 29, 40–42, 51, 81; asceticism of, 12–13; Buddhist community during his life and after, 19–20; death of, 21; deification of, 8; disciples

NOTES

History of Buddhist Humanism

History of Buddhist Humanism